HELEN EDMUNDSON

Helen Edmundson's first play, *Flying*, was presented at the National Theatre Studio in 1990. In 1992, she adapted Tolstoy's *Anna Karenina* for Shared Experience, for whom she also adapted *The Mill on the Floss* in 1994. Both won awards – the TMA and the Time Out Awards respectively – and both productions were twice revived and extensively toured. Shared Experience also staged her original adaptation of *War and Peace* at the National Theatre in 1996, and toured her adaptations of Mary Webb's *Gone to Earth* in 2004, Euripides' *Orestes* in 2006, the new two-part version of *War and Peace* in 2008, and the original play *Mary Shelley* in 2012. Her original play *The Clearing* was first staged at the Bush Theatre in 1993, winning the John Whiting and Time Out Awards, *Mother Teresa is Dead* was premiered at the Royal Court Theatre in 2002 and *The Heresy of Love* was premiered by the Royal Shakespeare Company in the Swan Theatre in 2012, and revived at Shakespeare's Globe in 2015. Her adaptation of Jamila Gavin's *Coram Boy* premiered at the National Theatre to critical acclaim in 2005, receiving a Time Out Award. It was subsequently revived in 2006, and produced on Broadway in 2007. She adapted Calderón's *Life is a Dream* for the Donmar Warehouse in 2009, and Arthur Ransome's *Swallows and Amazons* for the Bristol Old Vic in 2010, which subsequently transferred to the West End before embarking on a national tour in 2012. Her adaptation of *Thérèse Raquin* premiered at the Theatre Royal Bath in 2014, and was subsequently produced on Broadway by Roundabout Theatre Company in 2015. Helen was awarded a Windham Campbell Literature Prize by Yale University in 2015.

Other Titles in this Series

Mike Bartlett
BULL
GAME
AN INTERVENTION
KING CHARLES III

Deborah Bruce
THE DISTANCE
GODCHILD
SAME

Jez Butterworth
JERUSALEM
JEZ BUTTERWORTH PLAYS: ONE
MOJO
THE NIGHT HERON
PARLOUR SONG
THE RIVER
THE WINTERLING

Caryl Churchill
BLUE HEART
CHURCHILL PLAYS: THREE
CHURCHILL PLAYS: FOUR
CHURCHILL: SHORTS
CLOUD NINE
DING DONG THE WICKED
A DREAM PLAY *after* Strindberg
DRUNK ENOUGH TO SAY
    I LOVE YOU?
FAR AWAY
HOTEL
ICECREAM
LIGHT SHINING IN
    BUCKINGHAMSHIRE
LOVE AND INFORMATION
MAD FOREST
A NUMBER
SEVEN JEWISH CHILDREN
THE SKRIKER
THIS IS A CHAIR
THYESTES *after* Seneca
TRAPS

Helen Edmundson
ANNA KARENINA *after* Tolstoy
THE CLEARING
CORAM BOY *after* Gavin
GONE TO EARTH *after* Webb
THE HERESY OF LOVE
LIFE IS A DREAM *after* Calderón
MARY SHELLEY
THE MILL ON THE FLOSS *after* Eliot
ORESTES *after* Euripides
SWALLOWS AND AMAZONS
    after Ransome
THÉRÈSE RAQUIN *after* Zola

debbie tucker green
BORN BAD
DIRTY BUTTERFLY
HANG
NUT
RANDOM
STONING MARY
TRADE & GENERATIONS
TRUTH AND RECONCILIATION

Ella Hickson
THE AUTHORISED KATE BANE
BOYS
EIGHT
GIFT
PRECIOUS LITTLE TALENT
    & HOT MESS
WENDY & PETER PAN
    after J.M. Barrie

Sam Holcroft
COCKROACH
DANCING BEARS
EDGAR & ANNABEL
PINK
RULES FOR LIVING
THE WARDROBE
WHILE YOU LIE

Lucy Kirkwood
BEAUTY AND THE BEAST
    with Katie Mitchell
BLOODY WIMMIN
CHIMERICA
HEDDA *after* Ibsen
IT FELT EMPTY WHEN THE
    HEART WENT AT FIRST BUT
    IT IS ALRIGHT NOW
NSFW
TINDERBOX

Cordelia Lynn
LELA & CO.

Chloë Moss
CHRISTMAS IS MILES AWAY
HOW LOVE IS SPELT
FATAL LIGHT
THE GATEKEEPER
THE WAY HOME
THIS WIDE NIGHT

Paul Murphy
VALHALLA

Rona Munro
THE ASTRONAUT'S CHAIR
THE HOUSE OF BERNARDA ALBA
    after Lorca
THE INDIAN BOY
IRON
THE JAMES PLAYS
THE LAST WITCH
LITTLE EAGLES
LONG TIME DEAD
THE MAIDEN STONE
MARY BARTON
    after Gaskell
PANDAS
SCUTTLERS
STRAWBERRIES IN JANUARY
    from de la Chenelière
YOUR TURN TO CLEAN THE STAIR
    & FUGUE

Jessica Swale
BLUE STOCKINGS
NELL GWYNN

Helen Edmundson

QUEEN ANNE

NICK HERN BOOKS
London
www.nickhernbooks.co.uk

ABOUT THE ROYAL SHAKESPEARE COMPANY

The Shakespeare Memorial Theatre opened in Stratford-upon-Avon in 1879. Since then the plays of Shakespeare have been performed here, alongside the work of his contemporaries and of modern playwrights. In 1960 the Royal Shakespeare Company was formed, gaining its Royal Charter in 1961.

The founding Artistic Director, Peter Hall, created an ensemble theatre company of young actors and writers. The Company was led by Hall, Peter Brook and Michel Saint-Denis. The founding principles were threefold: the Company would embrace the freedom and power of Shakespeare's work, train and develop young actors and directors and, crucially, experiment in new ways of making theatre. There was a new spirit amongst this post-war generation and they intended to open up Shakespeare's plays as never before.

The impact of Peter Hall's vision cannot be overplayed. In 1955 he premiered Samuel Beckett's *Waiting for Godot* in London, and the result was like opening a window during a storm. The tumult of new ideas emerging across Europe in art, theatre and literature came flooding into British theatre. Hall channelled this new excitement into the setting up of the Company in Stratford. Exciting breakthroughs took place in the rehearsal room and the studio day after day. The RSC became known for exhilarating performances of Shakespeare alongside new masterpieces such as *The Homecoming* and *Old Times* by Harold Pinter. It was a combination that thrilled audiences.

Peter Hall's rigour on classical text became legendary, but what is little known is that he applied everything he learned working on Beckett, and later on Harold Pinter, to his work on Shakespeare, and likewise he applied everything he learned from Shakespeare onto modern texts. This close and exacting relationship between writers from different eras became the fuel which powered the creativity of the RSC.

The search for new forms of writing and directing was led by Peter Brook. He pushed writers to experiment. "Just as Picasso set out to capture a larger slice of the truth by painting a face with several eyes and noses, Shakespeare, knowing that man is living his everyday life and at the same time is living intensely in the invisible world of his thoughts and feelings, developed a method through which we can see at one and the same time the look on a man's face and the vibrations of his brain."

In our 50 years of producing new plays, we have sought out some of the most exciting writers of their generation. These have included: Edward Albee, Howard Barker, Alice Birch, Edward Bond, Howard Brenton, Marina Carr, Caryl Churchill, Martin Crimp, David Edgar, Helen Edmundson, James Fenton, Georgia Fitch, David Greig, Tanika Gupta, Ella Hickson, Dennis Kelly, Tarell Alvin McCraney, Martin McDonagh, Tom Morton-Smith, Rona Munro, Anthony Neilson, Harold Pinter, Phil Porter, Mike Poulton, Mark Ravenhill, Adriano Shaplin, Tom Stoppard, debbie tucker green, Timberlake Wertenbaker, Peter Whelan and Roy Williams.

The Company today is led by Gregory Doran, whose appointment represents a long-term commitment to the disciplines and craftsmanship required to put on the plays of Shakespeare. He, along with Executive Director, Catherine Mallyon, and his Deputy Artistic Director, Erica Whyman, will take forward a belief in celebrating both Shakespeare's work and the work of his contemporaries, as well as inviting some of the most exciting theatre-makers of today to work with the Company on new plays.

The RSC Acting Companies are generously supported by THE GATSBY CHARITABLE FOUNDATION and THE KOVNER FOUNDATION.

The RSC is grateful for the significant support of its principal funder, Arts Council England, without which our work would not be possible. Around 75 per cent of the RSC's income is self-generated from Box Office sales, sponsorship, donations, enterprise and partnerships with other organisations.

Supported using public funding by
**ARTS COUNCIL
ENGLAND**

NEW WORK AT THE RSC

We are a contemporary theatre company built on classical rigour. Through an extensive programme of research and development, we resource writers, directors and actors to explore and develop new ideas for our stages, and as part of this we commission playwrights to engage with the muscularity and ambition of the classics and to set Shakespeare's world in the context of our own. In 2016 we will re-open The Other Place in Stratford-upon-Avon, which will be a creative home for new work and experimentation. Leading up to that reopening we will continue to find spaces and opportunities to offer our audiences contemporary voices alongside our classical repertoire.

We invite writers to spend time with us in our rehearsal rooms, with our actors and creative teams. Alongside developing their own plays for all our stages, we invite them to contribute dramaturgically to both our main stage Shakespeare productions and our work for young people. We believe that engaging with living writers and other contemporary theatre makers helps to establish a creative culture within the Company which both inspires new work and creates an ever more urgent sense of enquiry into the classics. Shakespeare was a great innovator and breaker of rules, as well as a bold commentator on the times in which he lived. It is his spirit of 'radical mischief' which informs new work at the RSC.

Erica Whyman, Deputy Artistic Director, heads up this strand of the Company's work alongside Pippa Hill as Literary Manager.

The work of the RSC Literary Department is generously supported by THE DRUE HEINZ TRUST.

This production of *Queen Anne* was first performed by the Royal Shakespeare Company in the Swan Theatre, Stratford-upon-Avon, on 20 November 2015. The cast was as follows:

LADY CLARENDON	**Daisy Ashford**
ROBERT HARLEY	**Jonathan Broadbent**
JOHN CHURCHILL	**Robert Cavanah**
ARTHUR MAYNWARING	**Jonathan Christie**
QUEEN ANNE	**Emma Cunniffe**
COLONEL MASHAM	**Daniel Easton**
DR JOHN RADCLIFFE	**Michael Fenton Stevens**
SYDNEY GODOLPHIN	**Richard Hope**
SARAH CHURCHILL	**Natascha McElhone**
PRINCE GEORGE OF DENMARK	**Hywel Morgan**
ABIGAIL HILL	**Beth Park**
DANIEL DEFOE/WILLIAM III	**Carl Prekopp**
JEZEBEL	**Jenny Rainsford**
JACK CHURCHILL	**Elliott Ross**
LADY SOMERSET	**Anna Tierney**
JONATHAN SWIFT	**Tom Turner**
GROOM	**Ragevan Vasan**

All other parts played by members of the Company.

Directed by	**Natalie Abrahami**
Designed by	**Hannah Clark**
Lighting Designed by	**Charles Balfour**
Music & Sound by	**Ben & Max Ringham**
Original songs by	**Helen Edmundson**
Movement by	**Ann Yee**
Video Designed by	**Will Duke**
Company Voice and Text Work	**Stephen Kemble**
Assistant Director	**Jane Moriarty**
Music Director	**John Woolf**
Casting by	**Helena Palmer** CDG
Dramaturg	**Pippa Hill**
Production Manager	**David Tanqueray**
Costume Supervisor	**Rachel Dickson**
Company Manager	**Michael Dembowicz**
Stage Manager	**Linda Fitzpatrick**
Deputy Stage Manager	**Francesca Finney**
Assistant Stage Manager	**George Hims**
Producer	**Zoë Donegan**

MUSICIANS

Music performed live by

Oboe	**Graeme Adams**
Violin	**Ivor McGregor**
Cello	**Clare Spencer-Smith**
Percussion	**Kevin Waterman**
Harpsichord	**John Woolf**

This text may differ slightly from the play as performed.

THEATRE AT ITS BEST

Support us and make a difference

The RSC is a registered charity. Our aim is to stage theatre at its best, made in Stratford-upon-Avon and shared around the world with the widest possible audience.

We need your support and ask you to become a Member or join our Shakespeare Circle or Patrons Circle to enjoy a closer relationship with the Company. For just £18 per year you will receive advance information and enjoy Priority Booking for all seasons, giving you the chance to be among the first to see our new productions. For further insight into the Company and invites to exclusive events whilst directly funding the work on our stage join our Shakespeare Circle or Patrons Circle from £100 per year.

For more information visit **www.rsc.org.uk/supportus** or call the RSC Membership Office on 01789 403440.

THE ROYAL SHAKESPEARE COMPANY

QUEEN ANNE

Helen Edmundson

Characters

DR JOHN RADCLIFFE
ARTHUR MAYNWARING
DEFOE
JEZEBEL
ABIGAIL HILL
ROBERT HARLEY
JONATHAN SWIFT
JOHN CHURCHILL, DUKE OF MARLBOROUGH
JACK CHURCHILL
SIDNEY GODOLPHIN
SARAH CHURCHILL
KING WILLIAM III
PRINCE GEORGE OF DENMARK
LADY CLARENDON
LADY SOMERSET
QUEEN ANNE
COLONEL MASHAM
GROOM

And ARCHBISHOP OF CANTERBURY, LADIES,
GENTLEMEN, LORDS, MUSICIANS, PERFORMERS

*This text went to press before the end of rehearsals and so may
differ slightly from the play as performed.*

ACT ONE

Scene One

HARLEY's rooms. The Inns of Court, London, February 1702.
Various GENTLEMEN *are drinking and smoking. Here and*
there a WOMAN, *for the sake of titillation. In one corner,* DR
JOHN RADCLIFFE, ARTHUR MAYNWARING, DEFOE *and*
JEZEBEL *prepare for a performance. At* RADCLIFFE's
direction, a small group of MUSICIANS *strikes up.*
RADCLIFFE *steps forward –*

RADCLIFFE. Pray be upstanding for Her Royal Highness the
Princess Anne!

Enter MAYNWARING, *dressed, crudely, as Anne. He is*
greeted by cheers, whistles and laughter from the assembled
COMPANY, *who get to their feet.*

And for her estimable husband, Prince George of Denmark!

Enter DEFOE, *dressed as George. He bows, and makes a*
show of delight about the cheers that greet him. They begin
to sing.

DEFOE. Tonight?

MAYNWARING. Tonight it has to be,
I'm ripe as a cherry upon the tree,
Pray come and squeeze the pips from me,
We'll do it tonight for England.

RADCLIFFE *and* JEZEBEL *lead* MUSICIANS *and anyone*
who will sing in a chorus.

COMPANY.
So here's a cheer for Princess Anne,
She's doing her duty the way she can,
She's up and down like any man,
She's giving it all for England.

As the chorus is sung, MAYNWARING *and* DEFOE *as Anne and George, chase each other and then simulate copulation in a bawdy way. They sing again.*

MAYNWARING. Oh, George, Oh George,
I think I swell –

DEFOE. But Annie, my pudding, how can you tell?

MAYNWARING. I felt it move –

DEFOE. Then all is well,
But better make sure for England.

COMPANY.
So here's a cheer for Princess Anne,
She's doing her duty the way she can,
She's up and down like any man,
She's giving it all for England.

The whole room joins in the chorus now as 'George' chases 'Anne' – 'Come here, my little one!', 'Oh, Georgie!' He catches her and they start to copulate again.

MAYNWARING. Oh, George, come quick…

He does so.

I think I start…

RADCLIFFE *steps into the scene, brandishing a surgical instrument.*

RADCLIFFE. Lie down please, madam, and legs apart –

A cheer goes up from the COMPANY. *'Anne' lies down on a table.* JEZEBEL *makes a show of shielding 'Anne's' rear from view, using a sheet.*

JEZEBEL. Now brace yourself, for this may smart…

The audience love this. RADCLIFFE *ducks under the sheet to examine 'Anne'. The music creates a sense of suspension. 'Anne' begins to moan loudly – there is an ambiguity as to whether this is with pain or pleasure.*

HECKLER. Think of Hanover!

More laughter.

DEFOE. What news, good doctor, is she near?

RADCLIFFE. No head. No feet. What have we here?

MAYNWARING. It comes! It comes!

RADCLIFFE. Watch out! Stand clear!

'Anne' begins to make the sound of bearing down and pushing. There is a drum roll.

The Princess Anne,
God bless her heart,
Is now delivered of...

'Anne' lets out an enormous and protracted fart. This is met with cheers and laughter. The sheet is blown away.
RADCLIFFE, *'George' and* JEZEBEL *look as though they will be blown away too. The fart stops for a second or two, but then continues, until it finally stops.*

DEFOE (*mystically*). A fart.

'Anne' sits up.

MAYNWARING. Oh, but what a pretty one.

As the whole room sings the chorus, JEZEBEL *makes a bundle of the sheet, and puts it into 'Anne's' arms, as though it is a baby. 'Anne' and 'George' look at it, lovingly.*

COMPANY.
So here's a cheer for Princess Anne,
She's doing her duty the way she can,
She's up and down like any man,
She's giving it all for England.

'Anne' and 'George' dance and the song comes to an end. The PERFORMERS *take the applause.*

A woman (ABIGAIL HILL) has entered during the song and listened to the end of it. She looks about the room. She is exceptionally plain with pox-scarred skin, poorly dressed, with a woollen cloak about her. DEFOE *crosses in front of her.*

ABIGAIL. Excuse me? Is this… can this be the Inns of Court?

DEFOE. The Inns of Court it is. Though some might say we're better called the 'Outs'.

ABIGAIL. And are these Mr Harley's rooms?

MAYNWARING (*calling from across the room*). Defoe, your drink!

DEFOE *indicates a table to* ABIGAIL.

DEFOE. He's over there. (*To* MAYNWARING.) *J'arrive, ma chère!*

DEFOE *moves off and* ABIGAIL *crosses to the table, where sit* ROBERT HARLEY *and* JONATHAN SWIFT, *deep in conversation.* SWIFT, *as a clergyman, wears a dog collar, although it is presently concealed.*

ABIGAIL. Mr Robert Harley?

SWIFT. Who wants to know?

ABIGAIL. My name is Hill.

SWIFT. Hill?

ABIGAIL. Miss Abigail Hill.

SWIFT. Ah. Female then.

ABIGAIL. I'm sorry for intruding upon your evening, Mr Harley, but your housekeeper was kind enough to tell me I might find you here.

SWIFT. Had we an appointment?

ABIGAIL. No, sir, but…

SWIFT. Then you are here with some petition?

ABIGAIL. We are related, sir. On my father's side. Hill. Perhaps you recognise the name?

SWIFT. And this kinship you allege entitles you to touch me now for money, I suppose?

ABIGAIL. I'm not here to ask for money, sir.

SWIFT. Oh?

ABIGAIL. I've travelled from the country and am looking for employment. I wish to know if there are any jobs I might perform within your household?

SWIFT. Well, that rather depends, Miss Hill.

ABIGAIL. On what, sir?

SWIFT. On whether your arse is prettier than your face.

HARLEY *almost chokes on his drink.*

ABIGAIL. At least I keep my arse where it belongs, and do not choose to talk through it like some.

HARLEY. Hoo, hoo. I say!

SWIFT. Very good. That's really very good. You have a talented tongue, Miss Hill.

HARLEY *spies* RADCLIFFE *passing close by.*

HARLEY. Dr Radcliffe! A word, sir, if you will!

RADCLIFFE *approaches. He nods to* HARLEY.

RADCLIFFE. Harley.

And then to SWIFT.

Swift.

ABIGAIL *looks from one man to the other, realising she's been tricked.*

I trust you both enjoyed our little entertainment.

HARLEY. You are confirmed then in your opinion that the Princess Anne is not with child?

RADCLIFFE. The Princess is as likely to produce another child as you or I. Her age is now against her. And I have seen for myself, at closer quarters than I would wish, the damage done to her by all her pregnancies to date. Add to that the great bulk she carries presently about her like some fatty blanket, and I can say with certainty, no child will ever thrive within her womb. You may put that in a pamphlet, Swift.

SWIFT. Oh, I intend to.

RADCLIFFE. But no accreditation.

SWIFT. Naturally.

RADCLIFFE. Harley, I should ask your friends in Parliament to urge King William to wed again and quick, for there's our only promise of an heir.

SWIFT. The Hanoverians are salivating even as we speak.

HARLEY. England will be theirs upon a platter.

RADCLIFFE. Unless the Boy Pretender gets to table first.

RADCLIFFE *looks at* ABIGAIL.

Now I shall leave you to your… friend. Male or female?

SWIFT. Female – so she says.

RADCLIFFE. Ah. Pity.

He leaves them. ABIGAIL *looks at* HARLEY.

ABIGAIL. So *you* are Mr Harley?

HARLEY. Indeed, I own that name. And must make verbal recompense for the antics of my friend Swift. He is apt to be a little mischievous, especially in his cups.

ABIGAIL. You should rather apologise for yourself. I came here in good faith, a cousin to a cousin and did nothing in the least to earn your scorn. To think I was afraid to step inside this place. I thought I'd find a world so grand I wouldn't dare to raise my eyes. Instead I find I've lifted up a stone.

SWIFT. Excellent again.

ABIGAIL. Well, I'll leave you to your sport. And I thank God I'm not a princess, and need not suffer so-called gentlemen to make merry with my private sorrows.

HARLEY. Now, now. You mustn't take offence.

ABIGAIL. Why wouldn't I, when faced with liars and rogues?

SWIFT (*indicating his collar*). What, ho! Do you not see my uniform?

ABIGAIL. That? It qualifies you better for the charge.

SWIFT. You're wrong about our little 'club', Miss Hill. Gentlemen we may or may not be. Strangers to delicacy… now, that is certain…

HARLEY. 'Abandon taste all ye who enter here!'

SWIFT. But there's more honesty within these walls than anywhere in England. Truths spoken by we sidelong men tonight will tomorrow find themselves proclaimed in Parliament, decried from pulpits, printed up in black and white and spread through every street and town.

ABIGAIL. How marvellously important you must be.

Do you have a job for me, Mr Harley? Please answer yes or no. I'm poor, you see, and cannot run to pride.

HARLEY. Yes. Yes, I see. No. No. I'm afraid at present I cannot…

ABIGAIL. Then I will say goodnight.

ABIGAIL *starts to leave*.

HARLEY. Goodnight to you.

SWIFT. Goodnight, Miss Hill. Be careful with that tongue.

ABIGAIL *pauses and returns*.

ABIGAIL. Before I go, would you at least do me the favour of acquainting me with the current whereabouts of the Countess of Marlborough?

At the mention of this name, the whole room grows silent for a moment. HARLEY *grows immediately serious and direct.*

HARLEY. The Countess of Marlborough? Why, what can you want with her?

ABIGAIL. We're related on my mother's side. Perhaps I'll meet with better kindness there.

SWIFT. Now whose arse is holding forth?

ABIGAIL. I never lie, Mr Swift. It isn't in my nature.

HARLEY. But if you are related to the most powerful woman in the land, why choose to come to me?

ABIGAIL. I thought she wouldn't see me. Even now I doubt she will, but it seems I have no option save to try. Do you know where I might find her?

Pause. HARLEY *is calculating silently. He stands and offers her his chair.*

HARLEY. Sit down, Miss Hill. Cousin. Dear.

SWIFT. You cunning minx.

HARLEY. Drinks, over here!

ABIGAIL *moves to the chair, then hesitates.*

ABIGAIL. I won't be used.

HARLEY. No, no, I think that's clear. But where's the harm in trying to find some way to ease each other's interests? For family, let's say.

Scene Two

The bedroom, the Marlboroughs' house, St Albans. JOHN CHURCHILL, DUKE OF MARLBOROUGH *is sitting up in bed. His fifteen-year-old son,* JACK CHURCHILL, *is sitting on the bed. Both are in their nightclothes. In a chair beside the bed is* SIDNEY GODOLPHIN. *Standing on the bed, in a gorgeous nightrobe, is* SARAH CHURCHILL – *performing.*

SARAH. 'I am Sophia, Electress of Hanover,' says she.

JACK. But surely not like that, Mama?

SARAH. Oh, yes – for she is very old and German. 'And who might you be?'

'I am Sarah Churchill, Countess of Marlborough,' I replied, and shook my goddess curls.

'Ah yes – the General's wife,' says she. 'And how do you like The Hague?'

'I like it enormously,' says I.

'I understand you have the ear of the Princess Anne,' says she.

'I do,' says I, and would have said, 'I have her heart as well,' but I resisted.

JACK. You should have said it, for it's true.

SARAH. 'And pray, how is the Princess?'

Now… what to say to that?

GODOLPHIN. That is a question.

SARAH. For here's the woman in the world with most to gain from Anne's demise.

JACK. The very throne of England.

MARLBOROUGH. Tell them what you said, my dear. You'll like this, Godolphin.

SARAH. I thought – one second – then replied, 'The Princess Anne is as well as can be hoped, Your Highness – for someone who's so very sick as she.'

JACK. You're so clever.

SARAH. 'I understand,' Sophia replies. And by my life, she winked at me.

MARLBOROUGH. Did she indeed? You didn't tell me that.

SARAH. I liked her. She's the first woman I've ever met who can match me for intelligence. If England is to pass into her hands, I'd say we can rejoice. She may be seventy but she has more wit in her than William and Anne combined.

GODOLPHIN. This is good news. Did she stay for the signing of the Alliance?

MARLBOROUGH. She did. She stood beside King William throughout.

SARAH. Wearing twice her body weight in jewels. I promise you, Sidney, she's a woman after my own heart.

MARLBOROUGH. She's offered us twenty thousand men.

GODOLPHIN. As many as that?

MARLBOROUGH. Added to the Hapsburgs and the Dutch and our own, and I'd say that makes an army to command.

JACK. Are we really going to war against the French?

MARLBOROUGH. It's looking likely, Jack. The spring should see the start of our campaign.

SARAH. We go to war for freedom. We shall rid the world of papists and be thanked for ever after. And tyranny will never dare to raise its head again.

JACK. It won't be over quickly, will it?

SARAH. Why? Three years at least before you join the army.

JACK. No.

GODOLPHIN. You could always make a mascot of him, Marlborough – what do you say? Put him in a velvet coat, give him a painted drum to bang and send him out before.

JACK. I want to be a soldier not a clown!

MARLBOROUGH. One thing: the King has asked Sophia to come and spend some time in England.

SARAH. To set up Court, effectively.

GODOLPHIN. God's truth. Anne won't agree to that. And rightly so.

SARAH. She has no choice. We can't risk the future of the Grand Alliance for the sake of Anne's misplaced vanity.

GODOLPHIN. A little more than vanity.

SARAH. She may well die before the year is out – though we may pray she doesn't.

MARLBOROUGH. We thought to start for town at dawn. We'll speak to her before the King arrives.

GODOLPHIN. You must. Why, she'll reject the notion out of hand to spite him. That aside from all the quite legitimate concerns she's bound to feel regarding such a plan.

SARAH. How has she fared without us?

GODOLPHIN. Badly. This business with the baby has set her back considerably.

MARLBOROUGH. We heard of it.

GODOLPHIN. Though there's a pamphlet going round that claims there was no child at all – only a severe case of wind.

JACK. Really?

SARAH. I wouldn't be surprised it if were true.

MARLBOROUGH. Now then, my love.

SARAH. You men are far too soft about these things. But there. We'll set her straight tomorrow. Only you must promise not to leave me on my own with her. It's all very well for you – you talk a moment's policy then leave. I'm left to sit with her for hours. A morning in her presence and there are times when I could throw myself from the nearest window, simply to be sure that I'm alive.

MARLBOROUGH. You love her though – in honesty.

SARAH. Do I? If I do, I don't know why.

JACK. Can I come to London with you?

MARLBOROUGH. Of course you can.

SARAH. But it will mean an early start. To bed, my darling Jack.

JACK. Goodnight, Papa.

MARLBOROUGH. Sleep well.

JACK. Goodnight, Uncle Sidney.

GODOLPHIN. Goodnight, my boy. Start practising that drum.

JACK. I'll practise on your head!

SARAH. To bed now.

Exit JACK.

GODOLPHIN. I suppose I too should leave you. Unless there's room in there for a little one?

MARLBOROUGH/SARAH. Sorry, Sidney.

GODOLPHIN. Hum.

SARAH. But I can have a room prepared?

GODOLPHIN. No, no. I really should continue on to London.

MARLBOROUGH. We'll meet you at St James's.

GODOLPHIN. As early as you can.

GODOPHIN *starts to leave but pauses*.

The Pretender…?

MARLBOROUGH. Yes. We'd better write to St-Germain.

GODOLPHIN. I'll draft a letter.

SARAH. Goodnight, my dearest friend.

GODOLPHIN *regards her*.

GODOLPHIN. Marlborough – you're a lucky man.

Exit GODOLPHIN. SARAH *joins* MARLBOROUGH *in bed*.

MARLBOROUGH. Glad to be home?

SARAH. Exceedingly. But what a time it was. You were magnificent.

MARLBOROUGH. Was I?

SARAH. I watched you move around that mirrored room, advising kings and heads of state. And I thought, he's mine – thank God he's mine, that plain John Churchill, that brave and honest man. All those crowns, and only you are great.

None of them would go to war without you. None of them would dare.

MARLBOROUGH. There are many other generals.

SARAH. Yes. But none can honestly compare. This war will be your making. Your fortune and your fate.

MARLBOROUGH. Then it will be yours too.

They kiss.

Too tired, my darling?

SARAH. Never.

Scene Three

The bedroom, PRINCESS ANNE*'s apartments, St James's.* KING WILLIAM *(Dutch) is standing in the middle of the room. Behind him is* HARLEY. *In front of the King is a large bed, the curtains of which are closed. Standing close to the bed is* PRINCE GEORGE OF DENMARK, *half-dressed. Also present are two ladies-in-waiting –* LADY CLARENDON *and* LADY SOMERSET, *whose heads are bowed in deference.* WILLIAM *is addressing the bed.*

WILLIAM. A visit by the Electress Sophia to these shores will send a signal message to the world. The Protestant succession, together, side by side. It will leave the Spanish and the French no hope of any change in policy for years to come. And our allies with no doubt of our intent. With this you must agree?

Silence.

(*To* GEORGE.) Prince George, does your lady hear me?

GEORGE. Oh, yes, Your Majesty.

WILLIAM. Would she at least do me the courtesy of looking at my face?

GEORGE. Your Majesty, as I am saying, we are only just
    awake. My Anne is not now in her clothes.

WILLIAM. And what is that to me? Do you think I would be
    interested in that?

Slowly, ANNE *emerges from behind the curtains. She is
dressed in a shabby nightdress. She stays very close to the
bedpost. She does not look* WILLIAM *in the eye. She is full
of anxiety, fear and anger, and it takes all her mental and
physical strength to face the King.*

Princess. I hope you do not disagree with what I've said?

ANNE. I do not understand such things and therefore cannot
    comment.

WILLIAM. Tomorrow afternoon I will announce the invitation
    to the Court. All Ambassadors will be present. I ask only that
    you stand with me, and find your voice, and offer me
    support. May I count on you for that?

ANNE. I do not understand such things and therefore cannot
    comment.

WILLIAM. Why do you do this? This pretence of dumb
    stupidity? I know you understand me very well. And have
    opinions too. You're quick enough to speak behind my back!

GEORGE. Your Majesty, I must request, no shouting please.

HARLEY. Your Majesty, if I might make so bold?

WILLIAM *nods to him.*

Your Highness Princess Anne. Prince George. My name is
Robert Harley and I am Speaker of the Commons. I'm
gratified beyond expression to find myself admitted to your
presence. King William has asked me here today to offer you
assurances, and by your gracious leave, I will.

WILLIAM. Get on with it.

HARLEY. There are presently two Bills before the House. The
    first will make it treason to try, in any way, to prevent your
    Highnesses' accession to the throne. The second will attaint

the Boy Pretender, so that, should he ever dare to show his face upon these Isles, he may be executed without trial. These Bills will meet no opposition. I beg you to believe that there is no one in the House, nay, I might say in England, who has the slightest wish to see your claim usurped.

Pause.

ANNE. I am grateful for your words. Now I'm afraid I have to dress. It's almost time to pray.

WILLIAM. So what is your answer?

ANNE. I really cannot say. I do not understand such things and therefore cannot comment.

WILLIAM. This is impossible. I have done everything in my power of late to bring about a change in our relations. Have I not? When Mary died I thought that we had, finally, achieved some understanding. I lost a most beloved wife. You lost your only sister. I offered then, that very day, to be a brother to you – not just in law, but every way. Now I come to you today, from courtesy, and I am met with this. Intolerable.

GEORGE. Your Majesty…

WILLIAM. I begin to ask myself, yes, if you do not prefer to own the Catholic Pretender as your brother after all…

ANNE *flinches.*

GEORGE (*to* ANNE). My darling, I think what the King is trying to say…

WILLIAM. I do not need translating! Especially not by you!

Enter MARLBOROUGH, SARAH *and* GODOLPHIN, *alarmed.*

Marlborough. You had better speak to her for I cannot.

MARLBOROUGH. By all means, Your Majesty. I came with that in mind. A little late, I see.

WILLIAM (*to* SARAH). And you. Madam Favourite. I suggest you use your fabled status to show your mistress where her duty lies.

SARAH. I hope I can oblige Your Majesty. Though my mistress is all duty and needs no tutelage from me.

WILLIAM (*to* MARLBOROUGH). Come to me in Cabinet as soon as you are done. There is much we must discuss today.

MARLBOROUGH. Assuredly.

WILLIAM (*leaving*). Harley!

Exit WILLIAM.

HARLEY. Your Highnesses, forgive me.

My lords. My lady. Need I say? Colossuses of counsel. Paragons all three. Gratified. Honoured. Excuse me, if you please.

Exit HARLEY.

GEORGE. The King is quite impatient. I feel I must go after him and say some words.

MARLBOROUGH. Oh. Really, sir?

GODOLPHIN. I would leave him for a while, sir. Allow him to regain his equanimity. Whatever you choose to say at once will not be well received.

GEORGE. Ah, yes. Yes. Thank you, Lord Godolphin. This is good advice for me.

SARAH. Young Jack is in the stable yard, Prince George. He was hoping you would pick him out a horse. He means to join the hunt tomorrow morning.

GEORGE. My happy friend! Of course. I will go to him at once.

ANNE. A chair.

A LADY-IN-WAITING *takes* ANNE *a chair and helps her to sit.* GEORGE *rushes to her.*

GEORGE. Unless… My Anne. My little one. Would you rather that I stayed?

ANNE. No, no, my love. You go to Jack. You must.

GEORGE. Then I shall leave you with our dearest comrades.

GEORGE *starts to leave*.

ANNE. George? Don't forget to eat.

GEORGE. Ye gods above! I haven't had my breakfast. Is it not the pleasantest surprise to realise one owes oneself a meal?

Exit GEORGE.

MARLBOROUGH. Forgive us, my dear lady. We meant to spare you such a scene. A most unwelcome advent to your day.

ANNE (*slowly and tremulously*). I have no words unclean enough to tell you how I hate the King.

GODOLPHIN (*to* LADIES). Leave us, please.

Exit LADIES-IN-WAITING.

ANNE. Do you know his first remark when he arrived? He asked me why my rooms are decked in black? Why the black drapes at the windows? *Why?* Is there a woman on this earth with better cause to grieve? My father is not dead three months. Though he was exiled many years, do I not have the right to mourn? And I have lost another babe.

MARLBOROUGH. We know. News reached us in The Hague. We shed hot tears in thought of you.

GODOLPHIN. The country shares the burden of your grief.

SARAH. Indeed.

ANNE. But what am I doing? I haven't even welcomed you. Welcome back. Oh, welcome home. You cannot know how much I've missed you.

SARAH. We missed you too.

ANNE. But did you not receive my letters? I sent one almost every day.

SARAH. I had the last. Perhaps the others went astray somehow.

MARLBOROUGH. Sarah was in great demand.

SARAH. The girls and I were taken here and everywhere. To Ghent, to Amsterdam. We hardly knew where we would be from one day to the next.

ANNE. Your lucky daughters. If only I could have travelled with you too.

SARAH. How heavenly that would have been.

GODOLPHIN. Your Highness, if we might gently touch upon the invitation issued to Sophia?

ANNE. I can't allow it. Can I? It's done to make a fool of me. What, will she jump into my grave?

MARLBOROUGH. I'm certain that was not the King's intention.

SARAH. I doubt that he considered you. You're not so very major in his thoughts.

GODOLPHIN. Ma'am, your exiled father's death in St-Germain has precipitated something of a   crisis. As he took his final breaths, they say King Louis knelt beside his bed and swore to him he will not rest until he's seen his son…

SARAH. The Pretender.

GODOLPHIN. Yes – installed upon the English throne.

SARAH. And England is made Catholic.

MARLBOROUGH. That's why, ma'am, this Alliance is so vital. An alliance of Protestant sovereigns united in the solemn aim of defeating Catholic ambition.

Pause.

ANNE. But why should Sophia have to come here? She'll never wear the crown. Her claim is academic, is it not? The Dutchman's questionable reign is like to last for many years to come and then I will be Queen. And I will have a daughter or a son and he will then succeed me.

GODOLPHIN. Please God that it is so.

ANNE. And there's our Protestant succession.

SARAH. But we must consider all eventualities.

ANNE. The Dutchman dared to claim I love the Boy Pretender.
I, who have done more than anyone to disavow that
impostor, that urchin, who my most misguided father picked
up off the street.

GODOLPHIN. Yes, ma'am.

ANNE. And to say he came today from 'courtesy'. He does not
know the meaning of the word. He came because he needs me,
for there are those, there must be, who heed my actions still.

MARLBOROUGH. But of course there are, ma'am. That's why
it's so important that you give the invitation your support.

GODOLPHIN. Your Highness, as your appointed counsellor,
I'm bound to say I wish the King had spoken to you first.

ANNE. And so do I.

GODOLPHIN. But now the offer's made to her, I fear it can't
be taken back.

MARLBOROUGH. Not without we cause severe offence.

SARAH. Imagine how our enemies would jeer to see the cracks
appear so fast in our united front.

MARLBOROUGH. Even your silence at this time would shake
the people to the core.

ANNE. Really? I wouldn't wish unrest upon the land.

SARAH. Of course you wouldn't, ma'am.

GODOLPHIN. There is some Tory opposition to the war and
the Alliance. Your silence now would strengthen it, I fear.

SARAH. I think the invitation has to stand.

Pause.

ANNE. Very well. For all the world I wouldn't risk what
you've achieved. I'll go to Court tomorrow and support the
King in this.

GODOLPHIN. Thank you, ma'am. Your wisdom, as ever, is supreme.

MARLBOROUGH. I hope you know, Your Highness, that if any man were fool enough to put himself between you and the throne, I'd knock him down and trample on his guts.

ANNE. I doubt it not, dear Marlborough. And heaven knows there is no limit to my gratitude.

GODOLPHIN. I've written a letter on your behalf to the Pretender in St-Germain. As you know, it is our policy to placate the boy with false avowals of your consideration for his claim should you be Queen.

MARLBOROUGH. His advisers will have been alarmed by news of the Alliance. But a little reassurance should suffice to keep him fast upon our line.

ANNE. Then you have thought of everything for me. Just as you have always done.

GODOLPHIN. And will endeavour, tirelessly, to do so.

SARAH. Now we ought to leave you to your prayers. We know how much they mean to you.

ANNE. Thank you, my darling. But you'll return and stay with me tonight?

SARAH. Tonight? I can't. Forgive me. Jack soon returns to Cambridge and to his tutor there. I've had so little time for him with having been abroad.

ANNE. Well, then. I know too fully how it feels to crave some laughing moments with a son.

SARAH. I'll come back soon, I promise.

The MARLBOROUGHS *and* GODOLPHIN *move to leave.*

MARLBOROUGH. We'll see you at the Court, Your Highness, tomorrow afternoon.

ANNE. Yes. (*Pause.*) Hopefully.

They stop.

I dare say I'll awaken in the morning and find my resolution gone. Tomorrow will be very hard for me.

Pause.

MARLBOROUGH (*to* SARAH). Perhaps we could delay young Jack's return?

SARAH. Why, yes. I really think we must. I'll wait on you tonight, Your Highness.

ANNE. Will you, dear one?

SARAH. Happily.

Scene Four

A corridor, St James's. Afternoon. Enter HARLEY. *He looks about him surreptitiously. Enter* GODOLPHIN, *passing by from another direction.* HARLEY *tries to slip away, but* GODOLPHIN *has spotted him.*

GODOLPHIN. Harley.

HARLEY. Yes, my Lord Godolphin?

GODOLPHIN. Is Marlborough still in conference with the King?

HARLEY. He is, my lord. And has been so for many hours. I wouldn't hazard to suggest when they'll be done. Lord Marlborough's expertise, as you're aware, is unsurpassed. All hang on his authority.

GODOLPHIN. Where stands the Commons on the war at present?

HARLEY. Ah. Opinion's still divided. The Whigs are staunch in their support. The Tories though...

GODOLPHIN. How I hate this terminology. Must we be tribes?

HARLEY. Oh, I agree. The Tories though – and I hasten to assure you I am not of this opinion – fear the cost of it and wonder where it's like to end?

GODOLPHIN. Hum. Then we have work to do, Mr Harley.

GODOLPHIN starts to leave.

HARLEY. I trust to your tenacity, my lord, and will await instruction.

Exit GODOLPHIN. HARLEY *looks about once more, then exits briefly and returns with* ABIGAIL.

Now then. Wait here. She's soon to pass this way. Flatter her, but not excessively. She hates all manner of dissembling.

ABIGAIL. She'll find no insincerity in me.

HARLEY. Though I must remind you to conceal the matter of our kinship. She has no great aversion to me as far as I'm aware, and yet it might alarm her.

ABIGAIL. Then I'll neglect to mention it, and trust there is no lie in the omission.

HARLEY. But here she comes. You'll send to me?

ABIGAIL. If I have anything to say.

Enter SARAH, *in the company of* LADIES.

HARLEY. Countess, my lady, if you please?

SARAH. What is it, Mr Harley? I am rather pressed.

HARLEY. Forgive me for detaining you, but I found this woman in the hall. She seeks an audience with you but has been turned away, it seems, on numerous occasions.

SARAH. I expect there is good reason for it.

HARLEY. She is related to you, madam. So she claims.

SARAH indicates to the LADIES *to walk on. Exit* LADIES.

SARAH. Related to me? How?

ABIGAIL. My name is Abigail Hill, my lady. You met my
   mother once – your aunt – not many years ago. The kindness
   which you showed my brothers then remained with her until
   her dying day.

SARAH. Why, we are cousins.

ABIGAIL. Yes.

SARAH. You may leave us, Mr Harley.

HARLEY. Honoured to have been of service. Overwhelmed. A
   touching scene. Good day.

   Exit HARLEY.

SARAH. And so my aunt is dead, you say?

ABIGAIL. She is. I'm sorry not to bring you better news. I
   nursed her carefully to the end and felt it more than duty.

SARAH. I did the same for my mama. It is a daughter's honour.
   How might I help you, Abigail?

ABIGAIL. Ma'am, I own no more than what you see. I know
   you helped my brothers gain a foothold in the world, and
   though I lack all polish and refinement, am just a simple
   country girl, I hope that you might find it in your heart to
   help me too. I know your worth, and wouldn't ask were I not
   sure I'd truly be of service. I'm strong and have good hands
   and knees. There's nothing honest I'm ashamed to do.

SARAH. I see. (*Pause.*) Perhaps you know my father lived in
   debt?

ABIGAIL. I did hear tell of it.

SARAH. We scraped and crawled for money every day. And
   though I may dine richly now, I never will forget the taste of
   poverty. I set no store by privilege. My husband feels the
   same. A title handed down at birth does not ensure a soul's
   nobility. We judge on merit. It is our first and only gauge.

   I sense you have integrity.

ABIGAIL. I like to think I do.

SARAH. The Princess Anne requires a Woman of the Chamber. Such positions are not strictly my domain, but I can speak to Lady Clarendon on your behalf – she wouldn't dare refuse my protegée.

ABIGAIL. Thank you. You won't regret your faith in me.

SARAH. Come – walk along. And tell me more of how my cousins fare.

Exit SARAH and ABIGAIL.

Scene Five

ANNE*'s bedroom, her apartments, St James's. Night. ANNE is in her shabby nightdress. She is sitting in a chair. RADCLIFFE is on his knees before her, examining her legs. Several LADIES are in attendance, including her First Lady, LADY CLARENDON. At the back, near the door, is ABIGAIL. She now wears an apron and a scarf around her hair.*

RADCLIFFE. This swelling grows acute, I fear. There is a quantity of fluid the like of which I've never seen. The poultices must be applied and regularly.

LADY CLARENDON. As they have been, I assure you, Dr Radcliffe. We follow your instructions to the letter.

He manipulates one of ANNE's legs.

ANNE. Aargh! Unbearable.

Enter SARAH. She watches the proceedings.

RADCLIFFE. I think we want another change in diet. I'll talk to your cooks, Your Highness, if I may? Lean meat, a little fish perhaps. Certainly no cheese or cream.

ANNE. But cheese is such a comfort to me, doctor.

SARAH. In Amsterdam they start to say that walking is of benefit to gout.

ANNE. Countess. At last. Thank heavens. Take my hand for it is torture.

SARAH *goes to* ANNE *and does so*.

RADCLIFFE. Respectfully, my lady, the common quack is not confined to England. Besides, these symptoms aren't entirely typical of that disease. No, no. Rest and quiet are chiefly what Her Highness needs at present. All done.

RADCLIFFE *stands. The* LADIES *cover* ANNE*'s legs for her.*

ANNE. Thank you, doctor.

RADCLIFFE. I will return tomorrow night to check upon your care.

ANNE. And if Prince George should come to me again?

RADCLIFFE. Ah, yes. I'd recommend two weeks respite before resumption of your valiant efforts.

ANNE. Poor man. It's cruel. I know he craves me desperately.

RADCLIFFE. As well he might.

Now, if Your Highness will excuse me?

ANNE. Yes, good Dr Radcliffe.

RADCLIFFE. Your servant.

Exit RADCLIFFE.

ANNE. How tenderly he cares for me. What time is it?

SARAH. It's almost nine, Your Highness. I suggest that you retire at once.

ANNE. I will then.

LADY CLARENDON. What dresses will Your Highness be requiring for tomorrow?

ANNE. Oh, none, I think, Lady Clarendon. For I must stay in bed all day and rest.

SARAH. In the morning, certainly. But in the afternoon we go to Court. I hope you don't forget that, ma'am.

ANNE. Ah, yes. I'm afraid that won't be possible. For I am in a deal of pain and cannot face such ceremony. I think the matter needs must be delayed.

(*To* LADIES.) Unfasten me.

SARAH. May I speak to you alone, Your Highness?

ANNE. But of course you may.

SARAH (*to* LADIES). A moment.

Exit all, save ANNE *and* SARAH.

ANNE. What joy to have you to myself at last. I heard that Lady Harding forms a party to play cards. I feared that I had lost you to her.

SARAH. Ma'am, Marlborough has informed the King he may rely upon your presence tomorrow afternoon. I'm sure you know it's what we all agreed.

ANNE. It is a pity certainly. But look at me – I dread to walk…

SARAH. Then let them take you in your chair.

ANNE. I can't.

SARAH. I'll carry you myself if necessary.

ANNE. It can't be done. It cannot be. Forgive me but it can't. I will not stoop to please the King – that monster, that Caliban, that Dutch abortion!

SARAH. Quietly, I implore you. Pray, do not speak so openly.

ANNE. They say Sophia calls herself 'Hereditary Princess of all Britain', and that the King applauds it.

SARAH. Who told you such a thing?

ANNE. They say it's all around the Court. A vicious slight upon my name. Nothing would induce me to receive her should she come, so better that the matter's done with now and best they know it quickly.

SARAH *turns away from her and moves towards the door.*

Where are you going?

SARAH. You clearly have no need of me. You have the gossips and the fools to offer you advice, so I'll be gone and leave you to their counsel.

ANNE. What? No. Why, what do you mean?

SARAH. Your Highness, you have often said it is my honesty you prize above all else…

ANNE. It is…

SARAH. So I will now be forthright. I know it costs Your Highness dear to heed the King. But you must know it costs us too. Do you forget how cruelly he first used us? A full two months poor Marlborough languished in the Tower, and I was banned from seeing him. A long and dreadful persecution. And now we must submit to him, accept his tuneless overtures and sometimes, yes, admit he can be right. And this we do because we love our land and Church beyond ourselves.

ANNE. And so do I. (*Pause.*) But…

SARAH. Forgive me, ma'am. Goodnight.

SARAH *starts to leave again.*

ANNE. Wait! No. You promised you would stay with me.

SARAH. I've changed my mind, Your Highness – it's done so very easily. And perhaps I will not be too late for cards.

ANNE. Stop. Sarah. I will not let you leave me. I forbid it.

SARAH *stops in her tracks. She stares at* ANNE. *A dreadful look.*

Sarah. Dearest one. My darling… please. Forgive me. I will do this and anything you ask of me.

SARAH. You will?

ANNE. I'll go to Court, I swear it in God's name. I swear. But please don't walk away from me. I beg you. I'm begging you. I beg you on my knees.

ANNE *tries to kneel*.

SARAH (*stopping her*). No. Enough, Your Highness, please. I do not like to see you so distressed.

ANNE. Why do you 'Your Highness' me? Come – call me Mrs Morley. And I will call you Mrs Freeman and all will then be well again.

SARAH. I don't see how I can. We coined those names as levellers – to do away with hierarchy. And yet of late, I must confess, you've made me feel your status.

ANNE. No. Oh, never, never say so. You are the one half of myself. My equal in all things. And all the space within my heart which George concedes is homed and filled by you. Forgive me, Mrs Freeman. I would swallow daggers down before I would offend you. Forgive your faithful Morley, please.

SARAH. It's done.

ANNE. Then kiss these lips, as you once used to do.

SARAH. When we were girls perhaps. I'll kiss this head, and kiss these hands, and promise I am bound to you.

SARAH *kisses* ANNE.

ANNE. How weak I feel. Let's lie down side by side.

SARAH *and* ANNE *go to lie on the bed*.

It is the fear that makes me so alarmed.

SARAH. I know.

ANNE. I had the dream again last night. The hordes arrived and dragged me to the street. And forcing me upon my back they tore me limb from limb, and carried parts of me away, till there was nothing left of me.

SARAH. It is a dream and nothing more. You are secure within the people's hearts. Their true and only Princess.

SARAH soothes ANNE, *stroking her hair.*

ANNE. Sarah.

SARAH (*kindly in spite of herself*). Whatever will I do with you?

Enter ABIGAIL, *quietly.*

ABIGAIL. Forgive me, ma'am, I'm sent in for the pot.

SARAH (*quietly*). Take it by all means.

ANNE. Your hair is like a halo on your head. It's shining through my tears.

SARAH. I rinse it through with honey every day.

ANNE. It puts my lonely strands to shame.

SARAH. Hush now. Hush.

ANNE *is drifting off to sleep.*

ANNE (*whispered*). Stay with me.

SARAH. I will, my dearest.

ABIGAIL *goes to leave with the chamber pot.*

Wait, Abigail.

ABIGAIL *does so.* ANNE *falls asleep.* SARAH *extricates herself from her.*

Kindly make me up a bed.

ABIGAIL. Where, ma'am, if you please?

SARAH. The anteroom. The air is far too thick in here. I hesitate to breathe.

Exit SARAH. ABIGAIL *is surprised to see* ANNE *so abandoned. She goes to* ANNE *and covers her gently with a blanket. Exit* ABIGAIL.

Scene Six

The reception room, ANNE*'s apartments. Morning.* SARAH *and* LADY CLARENDON *are looking through a pile of* ANNE*'s dresses. Other* LADIES *and* ABIGAIL *are assisting.*

SARAH. Not this. Not this. Where have all her dresses gone?

LADY CLARENDON. Most of them no longer fit. What's left is what you see.

SARAH. A pretty sight she'll make before the Court. You should have ordered new ones made.

LADY CLARENDON. With what? She lacks the funds to pay for them.

SARAH. In truth, how can that be? I will not have her dressed so shabbily…

LADY CLARENDON. I hope you do not doubt me, Lady Marlborough. As keeper of the Privy Purse there's no one better placed than I to know the state of her affairs…

SARAH. Nor less to manage them.

LADY CLARENDON. Of late her stipend's rarely paid…

SARAH (*holding up a dress*). This! You jest. She wore this last when she was great with child.

Enter GEORGE, *breathless.*

GEORGE. Anne? Where is my Anne?

SARAH. She's in the bedroom praying, sir. But what's the matter?

GEORGE. I think I need to see her first.

SARAH. Did you not join the hunt today?

GEORGE. I did.

SARAH. Pray, what has passed? Where's Jack?

GEORGE. A bad and great calamity.

SARAH. To Jack?

GEORGE. To Jack? But no. It is the King.

LADY CLARENDON. His Majesty?

GEORGE. The King is fallen from his horse. His head is hit. His arm is all in pieces.

Enter MARLBOROUGH.

MARLBOROUGH. You've heard the news?

SARAH. Just now.

Enter ANNE.

ANNE. What's happening?

MARLBOROUGH. The King is gravely injured, ma'am. An accident whilst hunting.

SARAH. Is he alert? Awake, at least?

MARLBOROUGH. He is, but seems confused. I think we must go back to him at once.

GEORGE. I will come too.

MARLBOROUGH. No need, sir. The doctors are about him now.

GEORGE. But I should be beside his bed. He is bound to ask for me. It would be rude, I think, to stay away.

ANNE. I am not dressed.

SARAH. I'm sure you won't be needed, ma'am.

MARLBOROUGH. We'll send at once should there be any change. (*To* SARAH.) Come now. The Court is all in turmoil. We must control the story that is spread.

Exit MARLBOROUGH, SARAH, GEORGE *and all* LADIES-IN-WAITING, *save* ABIGAIL.

ANNE *thinks for a considerable time*.

ANNE. How strange this is. How unforeseen.

Pause.

ABIGAIL. May I assist you, madam?

ANNE. I had a son, a perfect boy, he lived to be eleven. And when he died I held his hand, and watched his soul depart his frame. 'Twas not a vision, not a dream, of that I am quite certain. I felt… I felt as I do now – suffused with God, awash with fate.

What is your name?

ABIGAIL. Hill, Your Highness. Abigail.

ANNE. It's only you and I, it seems. Help me down.

ABIGAIL *goes to her and helps her to her knees.*

Support my weight. And I will pray for kings, and queens.

ACT TWO

Scene One

Westminster Abbey. ANNE *is crowned Queen by the* ARCHBISHOP OF CANTERBURY. *She struggles to stand, under the weight of crown and robes.* GENTLEMEN *assist her to her feet.*

Scene Two

An anteroom, the Palace of Westminster. ANNE *is preparing to make her first speech to Parliament.* SARAH *is putting the final touches to her regalia. The noise of the assembled Houses can be heard. Enter* GODOLPHIN, *with a scroll.*

GODOLPHIN. Here it is. The final wording, ma'am.

ANNE (*taking the scroll*). Is it very different?

GODOLPHIN. A single line, that's all, reiterating the necessity for war.

Enter MARLBOROUGH.

MARLBOROUGH. Parliament awaits you, ma'am.

ANNE (*of the speech*). I think I need to look at it again.

MARLBOROUGH. I fear there isn't time.

ANNE. But… there will have to be.

MARLBOROUGH *and* GODOLPHIN *exchange looks with* SARAH, *who indicates that they should leave.*

SARAH. Ma'am?

ANNE. I don't know if I can.

SARAH. Speak as we rehearsed it. Stand straight and strong. You look magnificent. None could gaze upon you and fail to think of great Elizabeth.

ANNE. I shake.

SARAH. Mrs Morley. (*Hugging her suddenly and tenderly.*) My Mrs Morley.

Look at me. I confess, I think you have more courage than you realise. Remember the night your father rode out to meet William's invading troops, and we were forced to fly?

ANNE. Down the back stairs.

SARAH. Yes. I remember how amazed I was by your good humour. Your confidence. You even stopped to comment on the shabby paint within the passageway.

ANNE. I ordered it to be redone.

SARAH. I think you showed more courage then than I.

No one will expect you to be perfect.

ANNE. That isn't what I fear.

SARAH. Then what?

Pause.

ANNE. I want to be the fairest sovereign this country's ever seen.

SARAH (*surprised*). Well... that is a commendable ambition...

ANNE. Wait for me.

SARAH. I will.

ANNE. God help me.

Scene Three

The House of Lords. ANNE *addresses Parliament.*
MARLBOROUGH *and* GODOLPHIN *are amongst those who
watch. She speaks carefully and with effort, but in a
surprisingly clear, engaging tone.*

ANNE. My lords and gentlemen, I cannot too much lament my
own unhappiness in succeeding to the Crown so immediately
upon the loss of such a King, who was the great support, not
only of these kingdoms, but of all Europe. I am extremely
sensible of the weight and difficulty it brings upon me. But
as I know mine own heart to be entirely English, I can very
sincerely assure you, there is not any thing you can expect or
desire from me, which I shall not be ready to do, for the
happiness and prosperity of England...

Scene Four

HARLEY*'s rooms, the Inns of Court.* MAYNWARING,
RADCLIFFE, JEZEBEL *and* COMPANY *perform a song,
dressed as Sarah, Marlborough, Godolphin and Anne* [*roles
should be taken by company members as appropriate*]. *As
'Anne' gives away the various chains and keys of office, the
'Marlboroughs' and 'Godolphin' use them in order to ensnare
'Anne' and to turn her into a marionette, manipulated and
controlled by the chains.*

'SARAH'.
      Your Majesty, allow me please
      Your mighty troubles to relieve,
      The burden of your daily cares
      Will weigh less heavily once shared,
      The Privy Purse might fall to me,
      I beg you to bestow the key.

'ANNE'.
>   Oh take it,
>   Oh take it,
>   Oh take it.

'MARLBOROUGH'.
>   Your Majesty, allow me please
>   Your mighty troubles to relieve,
>   The testing business of the war
>   You need not suffer to endure,
>   I beg you to bestow on me
>   The key to matters military.

'ANNE'.
>   Oh take it,
>   Oh take it,
>   Oh take it.

'GODOLPHIN'.
>   Your Majesty allow me please
>   Your mighty troubles to relieve,
>   The machinations of the state
>   Are taxing to administrate,
>   The Government might fall to me,
>   I beg you, ma'am, bestow the key.

'ANNE'.
>   Oh take it,
>   Oh take it,
>   Oh take it,
>   Oh take it.

ALL.
>   Ma'am will you take it?
>   I will take it,
>   Ma'am will you take it?
>   I will take it,
>   Ma'am, will you take it up the?
>   Ma'am, will you take it up the?
>   I will take it.

'SARAH', 'MARLBOROUGH', 'GODOLPHIN'.
Your Majesty, allow us please
Your mighty troubles to relieve,
Authority in this great land
Is more than one can dare command,
The country might be ruled by three,
We beg you to bestow the key.

'ANNE'.
Oh take it,
Oh take it,
Oh take it.

The song concludes, to applause and laughter. ABIGAIL *has entered. Unseen, she approaches* HARLEY *and* SWIFT, *who are sitting at their usual table.*

ABIGAIL. They're wrong about Her Majesty.

HARLEY. Good Lord. Miss Hill. And here.

ABIGAIL. So it would seem.

HARLEY. You remember Mr Swift?

ABIGAIL. Regrettably.

SWIFT. All hail my acid friend.

HARLEY. But expand upon your subject, please.

ABIGAIL. I only mean the Queen has thoughts and leanings of her own. And in the weeks since she was throned, I've seen her try to stand her ground on numerous occasions, against the Earl and Countess. She has more strength of character than commonly believed.

HARLEY. What leanings then? Come, tell us more.

ABIGAIL. She makes no secret of them. The Church is closest to her heart – I never knew a person so devout. Prince George. The preservation of the Crown.

HARLEY. What else for me?

ABIGAIL. This isn't 'information'. They're merely observations, invited by the silly scene I saw just now.

SWIFT. Then, pray, what is it draws you back into our den of miscreants?

ABIGAIL. I need to ask if you will be so kind as to arrange my marriage for me, cousin?

HARLEY. Marriage?

SWIFT. Disappointing. How prosaic.

HARLEY. Why, to whom?

ABIGAIL. A Colonel in the service of Prince George. His Groom of the Chamber.

SWIFT. She aims her arrow high, at least.

ABIGAIL. His name is Samuel Masham.

HARLEY. Masham. Can't say I've ever heard the name.

ABIGAIL. There's no reason why you should have done. He's never loud and doesn't look for fame.

SWIFT. And does this shrinking fellow know the dreadful fate you plan for him?

ABIGAIL. Of course. We've talked together many times. I think that he's grown fond of me.

SWIFT. And does he see?

ABIGAIL. See what?

SWIFT. Why, anything at all?

RADCLIFFE *and* DEFOE *approach*. ABIGAIL *turns away – not wanting to be recognised*.

RADCLIFFE. So, gentlemen. News of the war. Tell them, Defoe.

DEFOE. I came past the Court just now and everything's astir. A missive from The Hague. It is anounced the Earl of Marlborough has been given charge of all the allied forces, land and sea. Commander-in-Chief and unassailable.

HARLEY. What? Surely there is some mistake?

RADCLIFFE. Not the King of Prussia, no, not Hanover, no not Savoy, not even good Prince George, but Marlborough it is who has his hands upon the reins.

SWIFT. Then we had better brace ourselves – he'll gallop after glory now, and never stop to look what's in his wake.

DEFOE. And those with land had best prepare to see it taxed to dust.

RADCLIFFE. Let's hope the Petticoat General has more to recommend him than his wife's allure.

Drink, drink, good masters, while ye may…

DEFOE. For tomorrow we are bust!

RADCLIFFE *and* DEFOE *move off into the room.*

SWIFT. They're gone, Miss Hill.

ABIGAIL. I ought to leave.

HARLEY. And so should I. There'll be some consternation in the House once this is known.

ABIGAIL. And you will speak to Colonel Masham for me, sir?

HARLEY. Yes. No. But why not ask the Countess to sally forth on your behalf?

ABIGAIL. I'd rather not increase my debt to her. Besides, I doubt she would approve the match.

SWIFT. Do I detect a hint of venom there?

ABIGAIL. You don't. I won't be drawn to taking sides. I simply have a life to lead.

SWIFT. Now, now – don't break my heart. You're surely not so green as that? The world makes politicians of us all.

HARLEY. If I agree to intervene and play a weighty cupid, what recompense do I receive?

ABIGAIL. None but my thanks. And if it helps, a private meeting with the Queen. We'd need to ask her blessing.

HARLEY *stops still, and his expression changes.*

SWIFT. Oh, God be praised. I think she's back.

Scene Five

Drawing room, Kensington Palace. Sunshine streams in through the windows, and birdsong can be heard, along with the occasional burst of laughter and shouting coming from the grounds. Enter ANNE, *richly dressed. She leans on* SARAH's *arm. Other* LADIES, *including* ABIGAIL, *are in attendance.*

SARAH. Perhaps I must repeat it, ma'am, for I fear you have not fully understood.

ANNE. But... I think I've understood you very well.

SARAH. The Earl of Wharton has to be retained as Comptroller of the Household, and keep his place in Cabinet. Seymour, who you think of bringing in, is a rampant Tory.

ANNE. Oh, how I do detest these new distinctions. I take no account of whether a man is labelled Whig or Tory...

SARAH. Then, forgive me, but you must.

ANNE. I simply do not like the Earl of Wharton. He's clearly a Republican. And nor can I abide the way he flaunts his mistresses about the Court. He offends my faith and everything I stand for.

SARAH. Good heavens! What a charge.

ANNE. Surely I must have men in Cabinet I can respect?

SARAH. Majesty. Your Majesty. I've told you this before – you needn't even go to Cabinet. Leave such business to Godolphin. No one would expect to see you there more than once or twice a year perhaps.

ANNE. It is my sacred duty to attend. Especially when we are at war.

SARAH. Is it not enough Prince George attends from time to time?

ANNE. You know the Prince has little heart for discourse. And now he has the Navy to command. Besides, he is not King.

Pause.

SARAH. We cannot lose the Earl of Wharton.

ANNE. Please. I tire.

SARAH. We must have a majority of Whigs.

ANNE. But surely we should aim to have a balance? Appoint the best and cleverest of men.

SARAH. Who puts these notions in your head? Ma'am, if you insist on favouring the Tories...

ANNE. I don't.

SARAH. Not only do you ring yourself with Jacobites...

ANNE. I can't believe all so-called Tories favour the Pretender.

SARAH. But you risk the fate and progress of the war. The Tories, ma'am, will vote it down.

Look – here is a letter from my lord, sent from the very cauldron of the fray. He's adamant that Wharton be retained...

Enter JACK *from outside. With him are* GEORGE *and* COLONEL MASHAM. MASHAM *notices* ABIGAIL *and goes to stand close to her. They smile at one another privately.*

JACK. Mama, you have to come and see. Prince George's dog is coupled to the chaise. I drove him round the grounds.

GEORGE. It's very small – the chaise, I mean. The dog is giant dog. It is a very funny thing. How are you, Countess? Is it not a lovely day? I hear brave Malborough takes another town. Bravo to him!

ANNE. The third he's captured on the River Meuse.

SARAH. And you, Prince George – I hope the burdens of the
Admiralty do not conspire to weigh you down?

GEORGE. Oh, no. No. At least… No.

JACK. Colonel Masham let me fly his hawk.

SARAH. And who is Colonel Masham, pray?

*MASHAM breaks away from ABIGAIL, who watches him
with pride.*

MASHAM. Here. Your servant, ma'am. I let the Marquess wear
the glove and taught him one or two commands.

JACK. Masham's with the Coldstream Guards.

SARAH. But clearly not at present.

MASHAM. Oh. No. A slight delay, I fear, with my promotion.
But…

SARAH (*pointedly*). And so you have more time to play. What
luck.

*MASHAM feels ashamed. He glances, uneasily, at
ABIGAIL, who feels his embarrassment.*

JACK (*to* GEORGE). Come on! Let's take the chaise around
again. (*To* SARAH.) Come out and watch me!

Exit JACK and MASHAM.

GEORGE. You stay for tea I hope, my lady?

ANNE. We're going to have it on the lawn.

SARAH. Yes, of course. And thanks.

Exit GEORGE.

ANNE. Kensington is such a joy after the confines of St
James's. And George's lungs are so much better for the air.
We mean to build an orangery, did I tell you?

SARAH. Won't that be expensive? I'll have to see the plans.

ANNE. But imagine having fruit upon the table, all fresh from off the tree. Do you remember when William and Mary first arrived, and invited me to dine with them? And William had the first peas of the season in a bowl in front of him, and ate them up, and never offered one to me, though I was desperate for those peas.

SARAH. Yes, I remember.

Pause.

ANNE. I hope my Mrs Freeman isn't cross with me.

SARAH. Cross? Why, how could I presume to be?

ANNE. You must come to me more often.

SARAH. It's difficult with Marlborough far away, and in such danger too. I need to be in Hertfordshire – my household doesn't run itself. Besides, I wrote to you three times last week to ask if you had need of me and didn't even warrant a reply.

ANNE. That can't be true.

SARAH. And yet it is.

ANNE. Oh, but I am mortified. Dearest one, you cannot know the great demands upon my waking hours of late. I hardly find an hour to pray. Why, last week I was entirely occupied with Scotland. We begin negotiations for the Union.

SARAH. I know. You waste your time.

ANNE. How can you say so?

SARAH. The Scots cannot be trusted. You should push them to agree to the succession. Nothing more. All else can wait until the war is won.

ANNE. But the Union will bring stability. And if you had witnessed, as I have, the colossal inefficiency of having two of everything…

SARAH. Did your negotiations work?

ANNE. No. But…

SARAH. Just as I thought.

ANNE. But I intend to try again and try again until it's done. But there. You must never, ever doubt your faithful Morley craves you. And you must always come to me, whenever you are able to. Let's go outside and have some tea.

SARAH. And the Earl of Wharton?

ANNE. I'll see the man. And I'll consider keeping him, provided he swears loyalty to me.

SARAH. But…

ANNE. What?

SARAH. I am surprised, that's all, that you insist upon the oath. It seems archaic – and better suited to King Louis's creed.

ANNE. All others now have taken it . And if he won't, how can I think to have him by?

SARAH. Very well. I'll speak to him.

ANNE. Thank you. Now. Let's go and watch the boys outside.

ANNE moves to leave.

SARAH. Might I speak with Hill a moment, please?

ANNE. By all means.

Another LADY goes to support ANNE. ABIGAIL goes to SARAH.

SARAH. I'll join you on the terrace, ma'am.

Exit ANNE and LADIES.

The key to the Privy Purse.

ABIGAIL hands the keys to SARAH.

Any unusual expenditure?

ABIGAIL. No, my lady. And everything is written down, as you requested.

SARAH. Thank you. You may go.

ABIGAIL moves to leave.

Abigail? Has the Queen had any private meetings lately, with anyone but Lord Godolphin?

ABIGAIL. Not that I'm aware of, ma'am.

SARAH. Please tell me if she does so.

Exit ABIGAIL.

Scene Six

The Queen's apartments, St James's Palace. ANNE *is finishing her correspondence for the day.* LADIES, *including* LADY SOMERSET, *are in attendance.* ANNE *puts her signature upon a letter.*

ANNE. Is that the last, Lady Somerset?

LADY SOMERSET. Yes, ma'am.

ANNE. Have them returned to Lord Godolphin's office.

LADY SOMERSET. Yes, ma'am.

Enter ABIGAIL *with* HARLEY.

ABIGAIL. Your Majesty?

ANNE. Ah, yes. Thank you, ladies.

The LADIES *leave.*

My cousin, Mr Harley.

HARLEY. Your humblest of servants, ma'am.

ANNE. I think I met you once before, sir. You are Speaker of the Commons, are you not?

HARLEY. I am. Why, that Your Majesty should deign to recollect the fact. Though it is not in that capacity I wait on you today.

ANNE. So I understand. Hill tells me that she has received a proposal of marriage, and from Colonel Masham of the Guards.

HARLEY. Precisely, ma'am. And as one dedicated to my cousin's welfare, I have spoken at some length with the aforesaid gentleman. He seems a fine and serious young man. But that which recommends him most of all, erasing the necessity for further scrutiny on my behalf, is that he holds the favour of Prince George. The trust and patronage of his most estimable Highness is more, far more than adequate to recommend a man to me.

ANNE. Thank you. My husband is most certainly a clever judge of character.

HARLEY. For my part, therefore, I am happy for the business to proceed. And so we come to beg of you Your Majesty's approval – nay, your blessing. For we dare to dream.

ANNE. I must confess, it touched my heart, and George's too, to learn that we had fostered love within our little home. Come to me, Hill.

ABIGAIL *goes to* ANNE.

If you marry Colonel Masham will you leave me?

ABIGAIL. No, ma'am. I hadn't even thought of it, nor would I want it either.

ANNE. Then I am satisfied. My blessing and my joy are yours.

ABIGAIL. Thank you, ma'am.

HARLEY. Your Majesty is gracious beyond words.

ANNE. I think you should be married in the chapel at Kensington. Unless you've somewhere else in mind?

ABIGAIL. We haven't, ma'am.

ANNE. And don't concern yourselves with the expenses – they are mine.

ABIGAIL. You're very kind, Your Majesty. Might I go and tell the Colonel? He awaits me in the hall?

ANNE. Then go to him. And bring him in to see me soon.

ABIGAIL. I will.

Exit ABIGAIL. HARLEY *dabs at his eyes with a handkerchief.*

HARLEY. Forgive me, Your Majesty. I am a foolish fellow.

ANNE. She is an excellent servant. I'm accustomed now to having her about me.

HARLEY. Ah, yes. She is a good and honest girl.

ANNE. Until she told me yesterday, I hadn't known that you are kin. It was Lady Marlborough brought her to me first. I wonder that she didn't look to her to make her applications.

HARLEY. Yes.

ANNE. Does Lady Marlborough know about the plan?

HARLEY. I… I cannot say, Your Majesty. I think… But there.

ANNE. Please tell me.

HARLEY. I think my cousin fears the Countess has no great opinion of Colonel Masham.

Pause. HARLEY *allows his point to land.*

And then, of course, that wondrous lady has so very many calls upon her time.

ANNE. She does. But I detain you, sir. I'm sure you must be wanted in the House.

HARLEY. I am obliged. The business of the day resumes.

ANNE. What do you debate this afternoon?

HARLEY. A further rise in tax on spirits, ma'am. And on malt, and hops. And coal. Tomorrow, I don't doubt the Chamber will be fraughter still, for we debate the rise in land tax.

ANNE. I hope the people fully understand, Mr Harley, the sound and pressing need we have to raise this extra revenue?

HARLEY. Oh, yes. Though there are some – and I hasten to assure you I am not of this opinion – who fear we ruin ourselves for the sake of the Dutch and other foreign territories.

ANNE. Ruin? Why, that's a most alarming word.

HARLEY. No, no, forgive me please. I'm sure that Lord Godolphin, as Lord Treasurer, is wise, and only too aware of how much extra strain the country can endure before she's brought, convulsing, to her knees.

Sincerest thanks, Your Majesty.

Scene Seven

ANNE*'s apartments, St James's. Evening. Enter* GODOLPHIN *with* LADY SOMERSET.

GODOLPHIN. Thank you, Lady Somerset. Do you know why I am summoned here so late?

LADY SOMERSET. I don't, my lord. The Queen is now at prayer. She's been a little agitated these last few hours.

GODOLPHIN. Is Lady Marlborough with her?

LADY SOMERSET. No. Though she was certainly expected here today.

Enter ANNE.

ANNE. Lord Godolphin. Thank you for attending me, and at this most uncivil hour.

Exit LADY SOMERSET.

GODOLPHIN. Is anything the matter, my dear lady? I hope you aren't unwell?

ANNE. No more than usual.

How much are we spending on the war?

GODOLPHIN. I beg your pardon, ma'am?

ANNE. I wish to know how much it costs.

GODOLPHIN. A not inconsiderable sum, as one might imagine.

ANNE. In numbers, if you please.

GODOLPHIN. In numbers. I... These are early days, of course, but my estimation for the expenditure this year is in the region of five and a half million pounds.

ANNE. And how much is our revenue to be?

GODOLPHIN. Somewhat less than that. But, as you know, we lately introduced a raft of measures...

ANNE. Taxes.

GODOLPHIN. Yes. To ensure the shortfall's not so great as it might otherwise have been.

ANNE. Why does it cost so much?

GODOLPHIN. I... I can hardly start to answer that...

ANNE. Our allies must contribute too?

GODOLPHIN. They do. That said, we are required to subsidise a certain few who...

ANNE. Subsidise? We subsidise our allies then?

GODOLPHIN. By no means all. We have to pay some foreign troops. I thought you were aware of this, Your Majesty. The subject has occurred in Cabinet...

ANNE. I clearly didn't understand. And pray, who do we subsidise?

GODOLPHIN. The Portuguese. Savoy. Hanover... .

ANNE. Hanover? Are we much richer than these other lands?

GODOLPHIN. No. Not presently. Not if one takes our debt into account. Ma'am...

ANNE. And if we cannot find sufficient revenue in months – or years – to come, what then? If the people cannot bear the burden of these fresh demands?

GODOLPHIN. It is my job to see they do. The war must be waged, Your Majesty.

ANNE. No matter what it costs?

GODOLPHIN. Yes. Louis crowns his grandson King of Spain. If Holland falls to their united powers, we are confronted with a vast, unbroken wall of Catholic strength...

ANNE. I know.

GODOLPHIN. How stop we the Pretender then? For he grows older every day and will see through our promises. How stop we any large invasion force?

ANNE. I know the need for our campaign.

GODOLPHIN. Has somebody alarmed you, ma'am?

ANNE. From now on I will attend all meetings of the Treasury.

GODOLPHIN. Good Lord. Forgive me, but that's unprecedented. Why, even King William did not...

ANNE. I do not care what William did or did not do.

GODOLPHIN. Very well. By all means please attend.

ANNE. I have to say, I start to feel I am not kept sufficiently informed.

GODOLPHIN. Of what, ma'am?

ANNE. I wish to be informed of everything, not simply of the business you're content for me to hear.

GODOLPHIN. Your Majesty… I hesitate to say I take offence, but…

ANNE. Please don't. It's not intended personally. But…

Enter LADY SOMERSET, *with a letter.*

LADY SOMERSET. Forgive me, please, Your Majesty, but this has come. They say it's more than urgent.

A letter for my Lord Godolphin.

GODOLPHIN *takes the letter. Exit* LADY SOMERSET. GODOLPHIN *reads.*

GODOLPHIN. Oh, no.

ANNE. What is it?

GODOLPHIN. This is dreadful news.

ANNE. Not Marlborough?

GODOLPHIN. It's Jack. Young Jack is struck with smallpox.

ANNE. Oh! Is it from the Countess?

GODOLPHIN. Yes. She's left for Cambridge. And Marlborough's on his way across the sea. (*Reading.*) 'Very sick' she calls him.

ANNE. I wonder that she didn't send to me.

He's such a strong and healthy boy. I'm sure he will recover.

GODOLPHIN. It's what she's always feared the most. I remember when he came to me in Newmarket – she made me promise not to take the boy to any other house at all, for there had been an outbreak in the town.

ANNE. I feel I want to go to her.

GODOLPHIN. And I.

ANNE. I'll write at once and ask her if she wants me there. And in the meantime I will send my doctors. And medicine. And any other help I can supply.

Scene Eight

St Albans. SARAH *and* MARLBOROUGH, *in mourning,*
process behind the coffin of their son, Jack. GODOLPHIN
follows behind them. SARAH *is being supported by*
MARLBOROUGH. *She stops and almost drops to the ground,*
overcome by grief. MARLBOROUGH *helps her to stand again,*
whispering in her ear. They follow the coffin.

Scene Nine

The drawing room, the Marlboroughs' house, St Albans.
SARAH *is sitting at a desk, writing. Enter* MARLBOROUGH.
SARAH *doesn't look up from her work.*

MARLBOROUGH. I leave in half an hour.

   I'll let you know when I arrive in Harwich, and which day
   I'm like to sail.

SARAH. Thank you.

   Pause.

MARLBOROUGH. Who is it you write to?

SARAH. The Queen. She asks again if she can come to me.

MARLBOROUGH. Perhaps you ought to let her.

SARAH. No.

MARLBOROUGH. She has at least a sense of what you feel.

SARAH. She has no idea. She didn't even cry when her boy
   died, but shut herself into the chapel with Prince George,
   praying. Praying. Thank you, Lord, for taking up my son.
   Thank you, Lord, for killing him. And walked about the
   court dry-eyed, all puffed up in her dignity.

MARLBOROUGH. I'm sure she felt it deeply nonetheless.

SARAH. Why do you defend her?

MARLBOROUGH. I only mean… that grief transforms our souls in different ways.

MARLBOROUGH *sits abjectly, struggling with his emotions.*

SARAH. She sniffs a chance to pity me is all. There is some tiny part of her is glad to know that he has gone. She never could abide the fact my children lived when hers did not.

MARLBOROUGH. I'm sure you're wrong.

SARAH. And far too many times of late, she's set herself above me. Or she's tried. Someone else has gained her ear, of that I am quite certain. Sidney knows – he feels it too. And now she thinks to push home her advantage. Well, she can stay away from me. I'll see her next when I am more than strong.

MARLBOROUGH *is silent. He covers his face with his hands.* SARAH *looks up and sees him.*

John?

They are silent for some moments.

MARLBOROUGH. Sarah, I'm afraid.

SARAH. No.

MARLBOROUGH. I fear myself – the first time in my life, I do believe. I fear that I'll regain the line and find I have no stomach for the fight. And that I'll question why I'm there. And what it's for, and what it means.

SARAH. That's not how it will be. He lives his life within us now. He multiplies our might. And when you fight, his spirit's vast within your heart. And every stretch of land you take, each victory, each new terrain, you plant a flag into the ground and say, 'This is my son.'

MARLBOROUGH *nods.*

And though I won't be next to you, don't ever doubt I watch your back, and wage our war upon a different front.

MARLBOROUGH *nods*.

MARLBOROUGH. Jack.

Pause.

SARAH. Let's go and see that they have packed you properly.

He reaches for her hand.

Sometimes he would pass me by and reach out for my hand. Just fleetingly, as though to say, I'm only checking you are there, for I am flying.

Scene Ten

Kensington Palace. Enter ABIGAIL *and* MASHAM, *hand in hand. With them is* GEORGE. *They are smiling and delighted with one another. Enter* ANNE *with* HARLEY.

ANNE. How beautiful a wedding is. I've never seen one yet and been unmoved. The daringness. The nakedness of hearts. And all the hopes of life exposed, and handed, gentle, to each other's care within the sight of God.

HARLEY. How sweetly put, Your Majesty. It was a perfect afternoon. They are a most devoted pair.

They watch ABIGAIL *and* MASHAM *for a few moments*.

ANNE. Tell me, Mr Harley, can you understand this fashion for what they term 'Occasional Conformity'?

HARLEY. Ah, yes. No. It truly is a scandal, Ma'am.

ANNE. Why do men deny themselves the solace of Communion? If I could, I'd take the Sacrament each day. And yet they take it once a year and think themselves quite clever for it. And think themselves quite fit to serve in offices of high responsibility. It is a loophole in the Test Act, is it not?

HARLEY. It is, it is, Your Majesty. But there's a move to have the practice banned.

ANNE. So I understand.

HARLEY. A Bill will shortly come before the Commons.

ANNE. Will it pass?

HARLEY. I think so, yes. Though I fear it will be savaged in the Lords – for there's a strong majority of Whigs.

ANNE. I want it to be known abroad that I support the Bill with all my heart.

HARLEY (*surprised*). I see. Consider it accomplished, ma'am. And if I might be so presumptuous as to offer a suggestion, Your Majesty might contemplate attending the debate within the Lords? No one then would think to doubt the strength of your opinion.

GEORGE *approaches*.

GEORGE. Anne. My Anne?

ANNE. Yes, Your Highness?

GEORGE. Masham asks if he might take his wife into the north to meet his family. Is this possible?

ANNE. I'm sure. When we're content to spare them both. I'll see that it's arranged, if it would please you.

GEORGE *returns to* MASHAM *and* ABIGAIL.

HARLEY. A pity that the new-made Duchess isn't here to share our joy.

ANNE. I thought it better not to trouble her. She struggles still to bear the loss of her beloved son. Since he passed she hasn't been to Court. Though we maintain a constant correspondence.

HARLEY. I imagine she must suffer some anxiety on behalf of her intrepid lord, the Duke. I hear he moves his army down the Danube and will confront Bavaria within her own domains.

ANNE. We are on tenterhooks each day awaiting further news of him.

HARLEY. Indeed. There are some Tories, I'm afraid – and I am not of this opinion – who say it is a reckless move, and that he gambles with a hundred thousand men. There are even rumours of impeachment should the risky tactic fail.

ANNE. I have the greatest faith in Marlborough.

HARLEY. Yes, of course. I merely felt Your Majesty would wish to be appraised of such disquiet.

Pause.

ANNE. Mr Harley, I would be obliged if you'd consider taking up a post in Cabinet. I find your counsel measured and unbiased.

Pause.

HARLEY. I hardly know what I should say. I fear I am unworthy.

ANNE. Then you won't?

HARLEY. No. Yes. I will, Your Majesty. And, on my knees, I swear to die or justify your faith in me.

Scene Eleven

The Queen's apartments, St James's. Two weeks later. ANNE *is sitting in a chair while* ABIGAIL *finishes dressing her – fastening jewels around her neck and a net of pearls into her hair.*

ABIGAIL. There's the bells in the cathedral ringing out.

ANNE. Yes.

ABIGAIL. And even now the crowds are cheering in the streets. They all await you, ma'am.

ANNE. How good, how kind the people are. I used to fear them terribly. Now I feel such care for them. Perhaps it is the suffering I've known, but I feel I would protect them from the harshest trials of life.

ABIGAIL. They love you very much, Your Majesty.

ANNE. Oh, there's such an aching in my bones.

ABIGAIL. Shall I send for Dr Radcliffe? It might not be too late.

ANNE. No, no. But were this not such a joyous day, I'd gladly spend it in my bed.

ABIGAIL. The bandages are quite secure – I've tied them extra tight.

ANNE. Thank you, dear. We wouldn't want them falling down. Now that would be a sight to see.

They smile. Enter SARAH. *She stares at them.*

Sarah. Sarah. Dearest.

SARAH. Good morning, ma'am.

ANNE. Here – let me embrace you.

Still beautiful. A little thinner, certainly, but…

SARAH (*of* ANNE*'s necklace*). Why do you wear that? I sent express instructions for what you are to wear today. I said the rubies.

ANNE. Oh. They didn't look so well as we had hoped. But if you wish to see them…

SARAH. Yes, I do.

ANNE (*to* ABIGAIL). Please fetch them, dear.

Exit ABIGAIL. SARAH *watches her go.*

Thank you for coming back to me. And on this day of days. How right it is that you should take my arm, and we should kneel together and give praise for Marlborough's splendid victory.

SARAH. I would not have missed it for the world. Though I hear we also offer thanks for some incidental skirmish won at sea. It rather makes a mockery, I fear, of Marlborough's feat at Blenheim.

ANNE. Not at all. We simply thought it would be right to offer thanks for all the efforts of our fine, courageous men. What the Duke of Marlborough has achieved is unsurpassed.

SARAH. History will judge it so.

ANNE. Please sit with me.

I want to give him an estate. In Oxfordshire, I thought. I know you love the country there. And we will build a home for you – a mansion fit for heroes.

SARAH. Thank you. But we do not have the wherewithal to honour such a life. It's hard enough that he is made a Duke.

ANNE. Then… let us put that right, and soon. I'll see he's paid a pension every year – a fitting sum. And I will raise your salary.

Enter ABIGAIL *with the rubies.*

Now then. Let's have another look at these.

ABIGAIL *begins to change the necklaces, one for the other.*

SARAH. I need to speak to you about the Bill against Occasional Conformity.

ANNE. Oh, yes? But surely not at once?

SARAH. You helped it through the Commons, I believe. I hope you will not help it through the Lords.

ANNE. But I intend to. Even George will vote for it and he a Lutheran.

SARAH. You realise that it's a Tory ploy to undermine our Government? A distraction from the business of the war?

ANNE. Really? It seems to me an urgent thing to have resolved. Men shouldn't be allowed to flout the right observance of our faith. And surely it is central to the meaning of the war? It is the Church we fight to save.

SARAH. There are very many Whigs who are Dissenters, as you know. This puts them out of heart. I say it is a matter better left to conscience.

ANNE. And mine dictates I must support the Bill.

We shouldn't talk about this now.

SARAH. When then? For I am not allowed in Cabinet.

ANNE. Another time. We don't have long.

SARAH. Another time?

I have been pondering of late, why it is you are so drawn towards those violent Tory lords. I realised that you imbibed their claptrap with your mother's milk...

ANNE. Sarah...

SARAH. I dare say you believe all Whigs are Roundheads, and weep at night for poor King Charles, who, incidentally, brought his fall upon himself, by thinking he was higher than the people he was meant to serve. And there's some irony, of course, for if your precious Tories had their way, you wouldn't be the Queen at all. The Pretender would be King.

Pause.

ANNE. I have a strong hereditary right. And I believe I reign with God's support.

Pause.

SARAH. Dear, dear. How serious we've grown.

ANNE. Mrs Freeman?

SARAH. Yes, ma'am?

ANNE. What think you of the jewels?

SARAH. I think they're better.

Pause.

ANNE. Thank you, Masham.

SARAH. Masham? That is Hill. I hope you do not lose your mind.

ANNE. Oh. She is Mrs Masham now. She married Colonel Masham of the Guards. We thought it better not to trouble you. And Mr Harley saw to the arrangements, so…

SARAH. Mr Harley? Why?

ANNE. He is a cousin on her father's side. (*To* ABIGAIL.) Is that not so?

ABIGAIL. Yes, ma'am.

Pause.

SARAH. Why was I not told of this? Harley who you've just appointed Secretary of State?

ANNE. Yes. I thought…

SARAH. I see. I wondered what had led you to that bacon-faced dissembler.

ANNE (*to* ABIGAIL). Leave us for a moment, please.

Exit ABIGAIL *to chamber.*

You needn't be upset by this.

SARAH. She is a servant – or supposed to be, and under my control. She clearly has designs on higher things.

ANNE. I don't believe that's true at all.

SARAH. How often have you seen your Mr Harley?

ANNE. I see the man from time to time.

SARAH. So now we know who's feeding you with policy of late.

ANNE. I beg your pardon?

SARAH. Do you have the least idea of 'Mr Harley's' politics?

ANNE. I'm capable of thinking on my own. And I resent this constant implication that I'm devoid of understanding…

SARAH. He's a Tory. For all his yes and nos. He is a Tory through and through. But that, I'm sure, will suit you very well.

Pause.

ANNE. Sarah. Mrs Freeman. I know you're grieving still…

SARAH. Don't.

Enter LADY SOMERSET.

LADY SOMERSET. The carriage is arriving, ma'am.

ANNE. Thank you. My cloak.

LADY SOMERSET *puts* ANNE*'s cloak on for her.*

(*To* SARAH.) Are you content to ride with me?

SARAH. Of course. Would I advertise our distance to the world?

ANNE. I…

ANNE *thinks better of saying any more. Exit* ANNE *with* LADY SOMERSET.

SARAH. Mrs Masham!

Enter ABIGAIL *from chamber.*

It seems I brought a cuckoo to the nest.

ABIGAIL. We didn't mean to cause offence, my lady…

SARAH. Your grace.

ABIGAIL. Your grace. We didn't want to trouble you, is all.

SARAH. What, you and Mr Harley?

You're very cosy with the Queen.

ABIGAIL. I… I wait upon her person.

SARAH. Has she tried to kiss you yet?

ABIGAIL. I don't know what you mean.

SARAH. But then again – perhaps she won't.

I have more history with her than you can dream. So don't you try to push me out. You lack the strength. You lack the wit.

SARAH *starts to leave*.

You have made an enemy.

Exit SARAH.

ABIGAIL. Very well, then. So be it.

ACT THREE

Scene One

The Inns of Court. Warning bells are ringing in the streets outside. Inside, a crowd, including RADCLIFFE *and* MAYNWARING, *has gathered in panic and alarm. People press around* HARLEY. SWIFT *is looking on.*

HARLEY. Gentlemen! Gentlemen! Let me speak, and I will try to answer all your questions.

Gentlemen!

SWIFT (*booming*). Quiet!

The crowd quietens somewhat.

HARLEY. I fear the news is true. A French invasion force is sailing from Dunkirk towards our shores and led by the Pretender.

Outcry amongst the crowd.

MAYNWARING. Where does he head?

RADCLIFFE. To Scotland I'll be bound!

HARLEY. He heads for Scotland. Yes. And at the invitation, so he claims, of many of our Scottish lords. He issued yesterday a proclamation calling 'fraud' upon the Queen.

GENTLEMEN. Scottish traitors! Hang them all!

HARLEY. But be assured… be assured, a fleet is sent to intercept. And Marlborough orders soldiers to the north.

RADCLIFFE. Too late!

GENTLEMEN. The Scottish troops will turn on us!

MAYNWARING. What about the bank? What about the bank?

HARLEY. The bank is safe. I swear to you. The Queen herself is sending a deposit as I speak, and Marlborough and Godolphin too deposit weighty sums. There is no cause for any great alarm.

Enter DEFOE *and* GENTLEMEN, *alarmed*.

DEFOE. The price of stock is tumbling! The goldsmiths won't pay gold!

Great alarm breaks out amongst the crowd again. Many rush to leave.

HARLEY. Gentlemen! Gentlemen! I urge you to be calm!

Scene Two

The Queen's appartments, St James's. ANNE *is waiting anxiously. Enter* MARLBOROUGH.

ANNE. What news?

MARLBOROUGH. It's over. It's over, ma'am. This time, at least.

ANNE. Truly?

MARLBOROUGH. Word has just arrived. They didn't land. Perhaps they grew uncertain of the promised help upon the shore. Leastwise, two nights ago, afraid of being trapped within the Forth, they sidled past our ships and headed back to open sea. But we pursued them. One of their vessels has been captured.

ANNE. The Pretender?

MARLBOROUGH. He was not on board.

ANNE. Then I thank God for that. For though it seems perverse, I'm sure, I wouldn't want his fate upon my hands.

MARLBOROUGH. Some of his most trusted lords are taken. Lord Griffin is amongst them.

ANNE. Lord Griffin.

MARLBOROUGH. And we move against those Scottish lords who helped to instigate the plan.

ANNE. When I was but a little girl he used to lift me up upon his back and run me round and round the Court.

What would they have done to me?

Enter GODOLPHIN.

GODOLPHIN. The word is out. The markets will grow steady now, I'm certain.

Your Majesty, I know the nation joins with me in giving thanks for your deliverance.

ANNE. Not all the nation it would seem. What mean the Scots? What is it irks them still? I thought the Union settled now.

MARLBOROUGH. Your Majesty, I'm mindful of the strain you've borne these last five days, and yet I feel compelled to speak. I am, perforce, so often far away, and I rely on Lord Godolphin and on my Duchess too, to appraise me of events at home. And more and more of late, the news they send alarms me to my core. The Jacobites in Scotland – yes, and everywhere – are given great encouragement by Your Majesty's espousal of the Tory cause.

ANNE. I...

MARLBOROUGH. They see the ruptures in our administration. They see the weakness there and they exploit it. And in the glens, or so I'm told, they whisper of your secret love for the Pretender, and say you'd rather have him follow you than any Hanoverian, for he is blood and kin of yours.

ANNE. But... that's absurd. I do not even own him...

GODOLPHIN. It is the Tory hope.

MARLBOROUGH. You block our strategy at every turn, reject each new appointment we request...

ANNE. I cannot think this crisis of my making. And I'm appalled that you should think it so.

MARLBOROUGH. Your Majesty...

ANNE. Mr Harley says this was a desperate ploy on Louis's part, a gamble, prompted by so many great defeats...

MARLBOROUGH. Harley?

ANNE. He thinks that we should move for peace whilst we are strong.

MARLBOROUGH. Harley's more the cause of this than anyone. His secretary is clapped in irons for sending secrets to the French – does that not ring alarms?

ANNE. But he has never implicated Harley.

GODOLPHIN. It happened in his office.

ANNE. This is what I most abhor. This posturing, this taking sides, this laying blame at other doors. You all are in my service, and I am in the service of this land.

MARLBOROUGH. He leads a faction now against us. And you should know the damage which that does to me abroad. Ma'am, I have to lead each new negotiation with our allies, each new and bloody fight, knowing that I have your full, unqualified support.

ANNE. You do.

Pause.

MARLBOROUGH. I wonder... if it would not be wise... for me to pause, and step aside.

ANNE. No. I will not let you do it. For if you did, you'd find it swiftly followed by another abdication. For what, pray, is a crown at all, when the support of it is gone? For Britain and for my sake, no.

MARLBOROUGH. I need hardly tell you what that means to me.

I must return to Cabinet.

He kisses her hand, meaningfully.

ANNE. Brave Marlborough.

MARLBOROUGH. Your Majesty.

MARLBOROUGH *glances at* GODOLPHIN – *unspoken communication between the two of them. Exit* MARLBOROUGH.

GODOLPHIN. It doesn't help that Sarah is so seldom to be seen at court.

ANNE. That you cannot blame on me. I've told her she can come to me whenever she is minded to.

GODOLPHIN. I think she lacks encouragement from you.

ANNE. I fear I cannot offer that. Although it mortifies my soul. For when she's here, she hounds me and berates me so. You've seen. And the letters she has lately sent are more than rude.

GODOLPHIN. I think she fears... that she has been replaced.

ANNE. Replaced? By whom?

GODOLPHIN. The servant girl. The one who's close to Harley.

Pause. ANNE *is shocked.*

ANNE. What nonsense.

GODOLPHIN. Is it, ma'am? Last week, when I arrived in Court, I saw the Swedish envoy in the hall. I asked him what he wanted and he told me he awaited Mrs Masham, for he would have her speak to you on his behalf.

ANNE. I never speak to Masham about policy.

GODOLPHIN. Perhaps. Yet...

ANNE. You doubt my word?

GODOLPHIN. Yet people think you do. And there's the damage done.

ANNE. This is beneath you, Lord Godolphin. I will not speak to you of this.

GODOLPHIN. Your Majesty, I am, or I am meant to be, your chief adviser...

ANNE. But you are not my father or my priest, and I won't be chastised, accused as though I am a wayward child. And I'd thank you not to write to Marlborough giving him false views about our dealings here.

GODOLPHIN. I cannot close my eyes and ears. Harley goes about the House speaking vicious lies of us...

ANNE. This!

Pause.

GODOLPHIN. May I suggest, for all our sakes, you rid yourself of Harley.

ANNE. Is that an ultimatum?

GODOLPHIN (*surprised*). No. It's simply my profound advice. As your counsellor and, I hope, your friend.

Pause.

ANNE. Thank you then. Good day to you.

GODOLPHIN *hesitates, uneasy.*

GODOLPHIN. I remain your servant, ma'am.

Exit GODOLPHIN. ANNE *is very still.*

Scene Three

A corridor, St James's. Enter GODOLPHIN, *walking. Enter a* GROOM, *a few moments later, a letter in his hand. He sees* GODOLPHIN *and rushes after him.*

GROOM. Lord Godolphin?

> GODOLPHIN *turns, and the* GROOM *thrusts the letter towards him.*

GODOLPHIN. Good Lord! I thought you meant to stab me, man.

GROOM. From the Queen.

GODOLPHIN. The Queen? But I left her not ten minutes since…

> *A realisation floods across his face. He takes the letter. He breaks the seal and reads.*

My God. You splice me then indeed, and through the heart.

> *The* GROOM *makes a small bow and starts to leave.*

Wait.

GROOM. She wanted no reply, my lord.

GODOLPHIN. But you had better give her this.

> *He takes the chain of office from around his neck and hands it to the* GROOM.

For I won't need it any more.

> *The* GROOM *leaves with the chain.* GODOLPHIN *is still with shock and sadness.*

Scene Four

HARLEY's *rooms, the Inns of Court. Evening.*
MAYNWARING, DEFOE *and* JEZEBEL, *in various guises,*
are performing a song to a delighted audience.

COMPANY.
Oh, the Grand Old Duke of Marlborough
He had ten thousand men
He marched them up to the top of the hill
And none came down again
And when they were up they were up
And when they were down they were down
And when they were only halfway up
They were falling on the ground.

Enter SARAH, *disguised in a cloak. She watches the*
performance.

'MARLBOROUGH'.
Say you, young man.

'OLD MAN'.
What me, sir?

'MARLBOROUGH'.
Why aren't you at the fight?

'OLD MAN'.
My heart is failing fast, my lord
And I barely have my sight.

'MARLBOROUGH'.
But flesh is flesh and blood is blood
And any now is meet
Come follow me I guarantee
You'll be finished in a week.

COMPANY.
And when they were up they were up
And when they were down they were down
And when they were only halfway up
They were dying on the ground.

'MARLBOROUGH'.
    Say you, young maid.

'GIRL'.
    What me, sir?

'MARLBOROUGH'.
    Why aren't you at the front?

'GIRL'.
    I have no skill for soldiering
    And my talent's in my… rump.

'MARLBOROUGH'.
    But some can fight and some delight
    And all must play their part
    Fall in, my dear, bring up the rear
    You can keep my weapon sharp.

COMPANY.
    And when they were up they were up
    And when they were down they were down
    And when they were only halfway up
    They were neither up nor down.

    Oh, the Grand Old Duke of Marlborough
    He had ten thousand men
    He marched them up to the top of the hill
    And none came down again
    And when they were up they were up
    And when they were down they were down
    And when they were only halfway up
    They were rotting in the ground.

The song ends and is applauded. MAYNWARING, *as its*
author, is warmly congratulated. SARAH *approaches*
MAYNWARING *as he divests himself of his wig.*

SARAH. Ingenious, I have to say. You have a catching turn of
    phrase.

MAYNWARING. Thank you, Mrs…?

SARAH. Churchill.

MAYNWARING. Do you know, you look exactly like... Oh, God. Your grace, I...

SARAH. And you are?

MAYNWARING. Arthur Maynwaring. MP.

SARAH. MP. Well, well. I might have known.

MAYNWARING. Your grace, I beg you not to take offence. It is a custom, nothing more, amongst we drinking fellows here to sing a silly, stupid... pointless, ill-judged and highly regrettable song from time to time. (*Falling to his knees.*) Oh, I beg, your grace, forgive me. I am a dolt, I am a fool, there never was a greater cur...

SARAH. Stop it. Stand up, if you please.

MAYNWARING. Why, yes, of course.

SARAH. I liked you better in your mischief, sir. Tell me, will you write a song for me?

MAYNWARING. For you? Oh, I'd do anything at all. And might I add, I feel... I feel as bold Odysseus felt, beholding first Athene in the splendour of her goddess form.

SARAH. I have heard fresher metaphors. But there. We'll work on that. Take me somewhere private, please.

MAYNWARING. Why, yes, your grace. Most willingly.

As MAYNWARING *and* SARAH *start to leave, enter* SWIFT, *who almost collides with* SARAH. *She sweeps on past him, but he has recognised her. Exit* MAYNWARING *and* SARAH. SWIFT *watches them go with great curiosity.*

Scene Five

The drawing room, Kensington Palace. ANNE *is sitting with* HARLEY. ANNE *is staring at a report which he has given her.*

ANNE. These numbers can't be right.

HARLEY. That was my thought too at first, and so I had them verified.

ANNE. Twenty-four thousand allied soldiers lost, and in one battle. How many of those men were ours?

HARLEY. Around six thousand, I believe. And yet we're told it was a victory.

ANNE. Marlborough warned me it had been a murderous fight. But this. I'd like to see a list of names – all those slain and injured.

HARLEY. Yes, Your Majesty.

ANNE. How will we replace them? Do we have any more to give?

HARLEY. The recruiting officers, so I understand, set about their work with zeal.

Pause. ANNE *is visibly saddened.*

I suppose we must endeavour to believe there is, indeed, no other course, but to ask this... aching sacrifice.

ANNE. Yes.

HARLEY. I fear I have some further troubling news. Since inheriting the Treasury from Lord Godolphin, I've found our finances to be in what I'd term a parlous state. The cost of war is spiralling. The bankers cannot lend us more – in fact they threaten to foreclose.

ANNE. Can they do that?

HARLEY. I'm afraid they can. I'm talking to them, naturally. And in the meantime, with Your Majesty's approval, I will venture to approach a certain number of financiers, private individuals who...

Enter SARAH.

SARAH. Mr Harley. *Quelle surprise*.

HARLEY. Your grace.

SARAH. I thought you would be standing by the gallows, sir. Your secretary hangs today, I understand.

HARLEY. He is my former secretary.

SARAH. It will be a relief to you to know that he is silenced.

HARLEY. No. Yes. He pays the forfeit for his treachery.

SARAH. I need to speak to you, Your Majesty.

ANNE. Thank you, Mr Harley. Please return as soon as you are able to.

HARLEY. Gladly, ma'am. And I will bring the list as you requested.

(*To* SARAH.) How goes the work in Oxfordshire? I hear you're building quite a palace there.

SARAH. It goes quite well.

HARLEY. Oh, joy. Good day, your grace. Your Majesty.

Exit HARLEY.

SARAH. I don't know how you can abide to have that odious man about you.

ANNE. How are you, my dearest Mrs Freeman?

SARAH. So he it is who takes Godolphin's place. The kindest man, the finest mind you have these years relied upon, is set aside for *him*.

ANNE. I hope my Lord Godolphin is not too greatly discomposed by his dismissal.

SARAH. He is bereft. He is aggrieved, and rightly so. He stays with me in Hertfordshire. I dare not think of him alone.

ANNE (*quietly*). All things cannot forever stay the same.

SARAH. What was that?

ANNE. I said, all things cannot forever stay the same.

   Pause. ANNE *is looking hard at* SARAH *now.*

SARAH. Marlborough is considering how he'll respond.

ANNE. I know. I've read his letter many times.

SARAH. I think it likely he'll resign.

ANNE. I don't. Marlborough will not leave the war.

SARAH. Did Harley tell you that? My God, he did.

ANNE. I thought it for myself.

SARAH. And what does Mr Harley know about my husband's state of mind?

ANNE. I think we ought to make a pact to talk no more of politics. Since I'm so unfortunate as to be unable to agree with you in everything, I fear we are condemned to argue, and it distresses me.

SARAH. Then perhaps you ought to heed me more.

ANNE. There are many other things we could discuss.

SARAH. Like what? The weather? Corsetry? Besides, I think you'd want to know what I have come to warn you of today. (*Taking a leaflet from her pocket.*) I came on this whilst walking on the Strand.

ANNE. What is it?

SARAH. A sort of rhyme. A song, in fact. It has a tune. A group of knaves was singing it and handing copies out to everyone who passed them by.

ANNE. If it is some cruel lampoon, I do not need to look at it.

SARAH. I think you should. For this one has a very potent sting. If you'd rather, I can read it to you, ma'am...

ANNE. No.

SARAH (*reading*).

> 'When as Queen Anne of great renown
> Great Britain's sceptre swayed,
> Beside the Church, she dearly loved
> A dirty chambermaid.
> Oh! Abigail – that was her name,
> She starched and stitched full well,
> But how she pierced this royal heart
> No mortal man can tell.'

ANNE. Stop it.

SARAH. But we reach the most disturbing part.

> (*Reading*.) 'However for sweet service done,
> And causes of great weight...'

ANNE. I said enough.

SARAH. Very well. Though I feel I ought to tell you that in a final verse it mentions some 'dark deeds' she does for you at night.

Pause.

ANNE. Why would anyone? Who would...?

SARAH. I know. It is abhorrent. We must accept, of course, such things occur, but to implicate Your Majesty in such a vile and sordid slur.

ANNE. It is libel. It is an attack upon my reputation.

SARAH. I agree. Though, I must say, considering the passion which Your Majesty's conceived for Mrs Masham, it's likely you'll continue to receive affronts of this unpleasant kind.

Passion... Masham. How curious – they almost rhyme.

ANNE *turns away, distressed.*

My darling Mrs Morley. The people are bound to be confounded – nay, disturbed – by the favour which you lately show that woman. And by her dealings too with Harley, who is mentioned in the song. And if you continue to divest yourself of old and faithful servants...

Enter ABIGAIL. *She is visibly pregnant.*

ABIGAIL. Forgive me. I didn't realise…

SARAH. Masham. We were just discussing you. Oh – I see congratulations are required.

ABIGAIL. Thank you, your grace.

SARAH. Do you start a dynasty?

ABIGAIL. I… No. It is my first.

SARAH. I'm afraid the Queen has had a shock. Perhaps you'd like to comfort her.

(*Holding out the leaflet to* ANNE.) Will you keep it, ma'am?

ANNE. Take it away.

SARAH. I will then.

SARAH *starts to leave, but as she passes* ABIGAIL, *she drops the leaflet, as though by accident.*

Oh. I'll leave you to dispose of it. Though I fear they are abundant on the streets.

Exit SARAH. ANNE *continues to look away.* ABIGAIL *picks up the leaflet and begins to read it.* ANNE *turns and sees her doing so.*

ANNE. Don't look at it.

ABIGAIL. Please don't worry, ma'am. My hide is thick. It's had to be. Shall I put it on the fire?

ANNE. Yes. I don't understand. Who would even… who would conceive of…

ABIGAIL. Ma'am, there's something I ought to tell you. And once it's said, I will forget I ever knew it, for I mean no trouble. Someone told me. The Duchess. She was lately seen conversing with the very man who's known for writing just such rhymes as these. I remember that I thought it strange. And now… This is so… singular. And I think perhaps… Well then. It is said and done. I hope it was the proper thing.

Pause.

ANNE. Leave me, Masham.

ABIGAIL. I'll stay close by, Your Majesty.

Exit ABIGAIL.

ANNE. Sarah. Sarah.

Scene Six

The drawing room, the Marlboroughs' house. Enter
MARLBOROUGH, SARAH *and* GODOLPHIN.
MARLBOROUGH *is dressed in travelling clothes. He is*
clutching some reports in his hand.

MARLBOROUGH. We're losing her.

SARAH. We're not.

MARLBOROUGH. Every letter brought me more disturbing
news. And these reports… Is there a Whig left in the
Cabinet? I wrote to her and almost begged for Sunderland,
yet still she will not have him.

GODOLPHIN. Harley's star remains in the ascendancy, I fear.

SARAH. But not for long. I am dividing her from Abigail, and
once that spotted strumpet's gone, I swear he'll quickly follow.

GODOLPHIN. I wouldn't be so sure of that.

SARAH (*to* MARLBOROUGH). But, my darling, you are
hardly in the door. Let me take your boots off. Come.

MARLBOROUGH *sits, and* SARAH *kneels and unfastens*
his boots.

MARLBOROUGH. The talk upon the front is all of peace. It's
madness. We need to take control of Spain. If Louis won't
agree to that… Why does she not see? We're battling a
hydra. We have to sever every head. We cannot quit whilst
one remains. Why does she not see?

SARAH. Because she has some sympathy, I start to think, with Louis's creed. Her High Church nonsense is only a step away from Popery. For all her protestations, she is secretly enamoured with divine right, and longs to resurrect it, and longs to outlaw any opposition.

GODOLPHIN. I really can't agree. Anne will never be a tyrant.

SARAH. No – because we will not let her be.

GODOLPHIN. It isn't in her nature. Granted, I've not spoken with her lately, but I cannot think…

SARAH. Sidney, you are too naive.

Pause.

MARLBOROUGH. Something must be done.

He stands and starts to leave.

SARAH. It must.

GODOLPHIN. But cautiously.

SARAH. The time for caution's past.

Exit MARLBOROUGH.

GODOLPHIN. He's exhausted.

SARAH *picks up* MARLBOROUGH*'s boots and goes to follow him.*

Will you tell him of the business with the song?

SARAH. No. There is no need to trouble him with that. The song will do its work. And quietly.

Exit SARAH.

Scene Seven

The terrace, Kensington Palace. Evening. Enter
MARLBOROUGH, *with* ANNE, *who is leaning on his arm.*
LADIES, *including* LADY SOMERSET, *are in attendance.*

MARLBOROUGH. The enemy was bearing down upon us. A
young lieutenant saw I'd been unseated and rushed towards
me with another horse. He held the reins. I put my foot into
the stirrup – and then it came.

ANNE. The cannonball.

MARLBOROUGH. Yes. And when I looked around at my
lieutenant... He was as close to me as you are now. Such are
the destinies of war.

ANNE. Surely you should stay behind the lines?

MARLBOROUGH. With respect, that would be a sort of heresy
in my regard.

ANNE. I understand. I pray to the Almighty every day to keep
you safe.

MARLBOROUGH. I count upon it, ma'am.

ANNE. Let's stay out here a moment. The evening is mild, and
we can watch the lights and the festivities.

ANNE *nods to the* LADIES, *who withdraw.*

I'm sorry that I've made you come away.

MARLBOROUGH. Oh, I have no heart for such diversions.
Not since... not since Jack died. And I'm glad to have this
opportunity to speak with you.

ANNE. I know that you're not home for long...

MARLBOROUGH. Three days.

ANNE. And there's something I must say to you.

The sound of music is heard.

The music starts again.

Prince George does so enjoy his birthday. And with it falling
on the leap year day, he waits four years for it to come
around. It makes me smile to think that in some strange,
official way, he's only twelve. And yet he's such a man.

MARLBOROUGH. Indeed.

ANNE. His lungs have been most troublesome of late. I must
confess, I worry for him. Sometimes it seems that both of us
are in the most decrepit state.

MARLBOROUGH. I fear we all begin to feel our years. Ma'am,
I have a most particular request which I would put to you.

ANNE. Go on.

MARLBOROUGH. My post as Captain General of our forces…

ANNE (*concerned*). Yes?

MARLBOROUGH. I hold it at your pleasure. But I've been
wondering if it would not be better were I to hold the post
for life.

Pause.

That way, our allies and our enemies alike will understand
that what I say is final and ratified by you.

ANNE. They should know that already.

MARLBOROUGH. Ma'am, I have decided to withdraw from
politics – at home, at least.

ANNE. My dear lord…

MARLBOROUGH. With developments of late, I feel myself
quite undermined and from so many quarters.

ANNE. But…

MARLBOROUGH. This way, I harness all my energies and
devote them to the business of the war. To our conclusive
victory. Of late, you see, I've realised that I'm a soldier –
nothing more. And the thought that my position could be
withdrawn, quite randomly…

ANNE. It wouldn't be.

MARLBOROUGH. And I hope you will forgive me saying this, but, God forbid, were anything to happen to Your Majesty, it would, I think, be best for all were my authority to stand through the ensuing change.

ANNE. I see.

Fireworks are heard. ANNE *watches them for a moment.*

MARLBOROUGH. I do not ask this power of you because I am ambitious – or covetous in any way. I trust you know that's true.

ANNE. I... I hope it might prove possible to grant you what you wish. Marlborough...

MARLBOROUGH. I've asked the lawyers to begin a search for precedents. That way...

ANNE. I'll give the matter proper thought.

MARLBOROUGH. Thank you. Yes. I couldn't hope for any more.

ANNE. It's strange that you should come to me with this and at this time. Perhaps we're both aware of certain shifts within the spheres. I need to ask you something too.

MARLBOROUGH. Anything.

ANNE. Oh, dear. If I dismiss your wife, would you resign?

Scene Eight

The bedroom, the Marlboroughs' house, St Albans. Night.
SARAH *is lying in bed. Enter* MARLBOROUGH, *quietly.*

SARAH. How went it?

MARLBOROUGH. Oh. Go back to sleep. I'll talk to you
   tomorrow.

SARAH. I wasn't asleep. How could I be? What did madam
   say? Will she allow it?

MARLBOROUGH. She means to think about it.

SARAH. That means she'll talk to Harley. You should have
   pushed her harder.

MARLBOROUGH. I couldn't.

SARAH. You should have got her word on it.

MARLBOROUGH. I couldn't. Go to sleep now. Please.

SARAH. What's wrong?

MARLBOROUGH. We'll talk of it tomorrow.

SARAH. What's the matter? John? John?

   Pause.

MARLBOROUGH. She wants the key. She wants you gone
   from all your posts within her household.

   Pause.

SARAH. She is dismissing me?

MARLBOROUGH. I tried to talk her from it, but she would not
   be moved. I'm sorry.

SARAH. I feel sick.

MARLBOROUGH. Sarah...

SARAH. Did you resign?

MARLBOROUGH. I... I thought it better not to. Not at
   present. If I resign... we're done. We're done.

SARAH. But she would not accept your resignation. She would reinstate me.

MARLBOROUGH. No, she wouldn't. Believe me. She is different now. This is an Anne who knows she's Queen. She'd let me go.

SARAH. No.

MARLBOROUGH. She would. Sarah. My sweetest love…

SARAH *shrugs him off and moves away.*

Perhaps it's for the best. You two have fought so much of late…

SARAH. Why? What reason did she use to fob you off? Except that Mrs Masham now resides within my place?

MARLBOROUGH. She said you'd done and said some things of late she can't forgive. Have you? What has passed? Has something happened which…?

SARAH. Forgive? That's rich. Forgive? After what she's done to me. Casting me aside, replacing me, and with a whore.

MARLBOROUGH. Sarah…

SARAH. My God, this is a farce. All those years of serving her. Of making her seem better than she is. I am so much more than her.

Enter GODOLPHIN.

I hate her. With all my body and my soul.

MARLBOROUGH. She is our Queen.

SARAH. And what of that? What are kings and queens but words? And if there is a God, I'm sure he laughs at us on earth for setting up such effigies. We're masters of ourselves. And we should look to none but those with proper strength and proper worth. No one is more relevant than me!

MARLBOROUGH. Sarah…

SARAH. What is she? What? A lump. A mewling grub that cannot even gurgitate an heir!

GODOLPHIN. What in Christ's name…?

MARLBOROUGH. She doesn't mean it.

SARAH rushes to the dressing table, where lies her key of office.

SARAH. Take it! She wants her… precious key! Take it to her!

MARLBOROUGH. I'll take it in the morning. Please…

SARAH. Now! Now! And take her this –

SARAH takes up a pair of scissors and cuts at her hair.

So she can see what she has done.

MARLBOROUGH. No!

MARLBOROUGH and GODOLPHIN rush to stop her.

No! Sarah!

A large bundle of her hair falls to the floor.
MARLBOROUGH snatches the scissors from her. They are quiet for a moment. Shocked.

SARAH. She will regret this.

MARLBOROUGH. I'm sure she will. You're right. But…

SARAH. And you'll regret it too.

GODOLPHIN. This isn't Marlborough's fault. She…

SARAH. She has divided us.

MARLBOROUGH. No. No. I begged her for you on my knees…

SARAH. You think that makes it better?

Take it to her now. I want it done. Take it to your precious Queen.

Exit SARAH.

ACT FOUR

Scene One

The drawing room, the Marlboroughs' house, St Albans. Letters cover the desk and the surrounding floor. SARAH *and* MAYNWARING *are amongst them.* SARAH *has a letter in her hand.*

SARAH (*reading*). 'But as long as I live, I must be endeavouring to show that never anybody had a sincerer passion for another than I have for my dear, dear, Mrs Freeman.' You see – she was obsessed with me. She couldn't bear to have me from her sight.

MAYNWARING. There's certainly some evidence of... rampant femininity.

SARAH (*reading from another letter*). 'Farewell my dear, dear life. I am, if it be possible, more than ever yours.' (*Reading from another.*) 'You'll never find in all the search of love a heart like mine, so truly, so entirely without reserve, nor so passionately yours.' Ugh! Now it makes my stomach turn.

MAYNWARING. My life, but what a scandal it would cause if even one of these were seen.

SARAH. You think that I should publish them?

MAYNWARING. Oh. Publish them? I didn't mean...

SARAH. No, no. I must confess, the thought's already crossed my mind.

MAYNWARING. I didn't mean exactly... God. But really? Would you dare?

SARAH. Why not? Don't people have a right to know the secret nature of their Queen?

MAYNWARING. Yes, but... Surely...?

SARAH. Perhaps I will, perhaps I won't. But at the very least, I think, I'll use the threat to frighten her. A clear but carefully worded hint should be enough. The thought of it will make her scream.

Enter GODOLPHIN.

GODOLPHIN. The thought of what?

SARAH (*indicating the letters*). These and these and these are all from her. Written to me through the years. There's some of them you'd blush to read. Maynwaring just pointed out how interested the world would be to know how passionately I was once adored.

MAYNWARING. I didn't say... I didn't quite exactly mean...

GODOLPHIN. Leave us for a moment, sir.

MAYNWARING *starts to leave*.

SARAH. Don't go away entirely. I might have further use for you.

MAYNWARING. Madam, I await your call.

Exit MAYNWARING.

GODOLPHIN. What are you thinking, Sarah? These antics will not help at all.

SARAH. Don't begin to lecture me, I am not in the mood.

GODOLPHIN. Why do you not write to her? Apologise and humbly...

SARAH. I will do nothing of the sort.

GODOLPHIN. You must be clever now. Show to her a milder form and she might call you back to her.

SARAH. I'm writing her a history. Already – look – (*Showing letter.*) it's thirteen pages long. The tale of our relationship from when we met as almost girls until this sad and sorry day. And laying out, impeccably, the services I've done for her, and all the promises she made. And not just those of never-ending love. She promised me that I would have those

offices for life. She promised, were I fated to resign, that
they would then be shared amongst my daughters. She swore
to me that she would pay for all the building work in
Oxfordshire. It's here in writing somewhere. I will find it, for
there's another oath she has reneged upon.

GODOLPHIN. But this will rile her further. Sarah, for your
own dear sake, if not for Marlborough's, take a more
conciliatory line.

SARAH. John's relationship with her is his concern. And none
of mine. Besides, she'll never break with him, for he's her
man. A hero for our time.

GODOLPHIN. I see I cannot reason with you.

SARAH. She must be made to face the wrong she's done. And
even someone burdened as she is with such a deficit of brain,
must read this and begin to see that I am used unfairly.

GODOLPHIN. I must confess, I do not like to hear you
speaking of her so.

SARAH. Why? Will you haul me up for treason?

GODOLPHIN. You hurt yourself as much as her to say such
things. We've all been fond of her.

SARAH. It was pretence on my part.

GODOLPHIN. That isn't true. As well you know. No matter
what you think about her now, she's been your greatest
friend. She has loved you most devotedly.

SARAH. Devotion can be irksome.

GODOLPHIN. But you would not have wished yourself
without it. Would you? Her care of you? Her constant
generosity?

Pause. SARAH *cannot deny this. She struggles to contain
her emotions.*

SARAH. That's why I am reminding her of everything we've
shared.

GODOLPHIN. Change the tone of what you write. Ask her for another chance.

SARAH. Did you?

GODOLPHIN. Well… no. But that was different. That was politics.

SARAH. Then nor will I. For so is this.

Scene Two

The Queen's apartments, St James's. ANNE, seated, looks sick and unkempt. ABIGAIL is beside her, wearing the keys to the purse and to the chamber around her neck. HARLEY stands before her. ANNE has a bundle of papers – SARAH's latest and longest letter – in her lap.

HARLEY. To publish them? But surely not? She cannot be in earnest.

ANNE. The inference is very clear.

HARLEY. Might I be allowed to see exactly what she writes?

ANNE. It is too personal, I fear. But Masham's seen.

ABIGAIL. The threat is unmistakable. She implies she will not hesitate to act unless Her Majesty recalls to mind her 'great responsibilities'.

HARLEY. I've simply never heard the like. You say the letters could be compromising?

ANNE. Yes.

HARLEY. Politically?

ANNE. Yes. In many ways. You understand – we sometimes put in writing things we'd hesitate to say.

HARLEY. This is outrageous. Your private correspondence. I wonder if it is not tantamount to treason.

ANNE. What do you suggest I do? I thought I would appeal to Marlborough first...

HARLEY. Don't. I mean... forgive me, please, but we cannot know the Duke himself does not concur and back this most audacious plan.

ANNE. What? No. No, no. He wouldn't, I am certain.

HARLEY. Yes. No. Perhaps. Allow me to be frank. There are those in Parliament who feel – and I hasten to assure you I am not of this opinion – that Marlborough's last request to you concerning the Captain Generalcy is dangerous, nay, obscene in its ambition. The lawyers search for precedents but none have yet been found. Save Cromwell. I won't offend the royal ears by speaking any more of him. But words such as 'dictatorship' are being whispered round. And now the Duchess seeks to undermine Your Majesty within the people's hearts. Besides all this, I'm sorry to report, that we begin to find some troubling anomalies in Marlborough's costing of supplies. Money being drawn aside. So one might say – I hope you see – a picture is emerging.

Pause. ANNE *is shocked.*

Here is what I would advise: send a short, perfunctory reply unto the Duchess, acknowledging receipt of her... epistle. Suggest you will consider what she's said. That buys us time.

ANNE. These anomalies you speak of...?

HARLEY. Yes. I will report to you again once I know more. Suffice to say, he would not be the only General, or the first, to make financial profit from a war. And some suggest that's why he won't have peace. Though the last proposals from the French are clearly worth considering.

ANNE. He says that Spain is still the sticking point.

HARLEY. Does he? Well. Perhaps. I'm sure.

But I should leave – for you are shocked and weary, ma'am. Might I ask, do you have in your possession any other letters from the Duchess?

ANNE. None save this. For I was careful to destroy them all. It's what we always promised we would do.

Pause. ANNE *grows tearful.*

HARLEY. Of course. Please keep that one, as evidence.

ANNE. Forgive me. I am so grateful for your help and your discretion.

HARLEY. Leave all to me. I swear to you, those letters will not see the light of day.

Scene Three

A passageway, St James's. ABIGAIL *is accompanying* HARLEY *to the door. They speak quietly.*

ABIGAIL. I'd say they've overreached their strength.

HARLEY. They have. And it is wonderful.

ABIGAIL. What will you do?

HARLEY. I'll call them out. Swift will be my second. She chooses print – all well and good – I'll let them have it hard between the eyes. Oh, yes. Stand by. We'll write them both to death.

ABIGAIL. Please do it quick. I never saw the Queen so frail. Prince George is ailing badly…

HARLEY. Is he indeed?

ABIGAIL. Now this on top of all. She almost fainted when she read the letter first. Then wept, and cried out over and again, 'betrayed'.

HARLEY. It's up to you to soothe her. And seize all opportunity to urge her to consider peace.

ABIGAIL. I cannot speak to her of politics. I've told you that. It would destroy her trust in me.

HARLEY. Then do your best. For heaven knows we must prevail.

Exit HARLEY.

Scene Four

ANNE*'s bedroom, St James's. Evening.* ANNE *is sitting on the bed.* ABIGAIL *is strapping up her knees, having applied ointment.*

ANNE. Are they very swollen?

ABIGAIL. They are.

ANNE. I cannot bear to look at them these days.

ABIGAIL. The doctor comes again tomorrow morning. We'll get you well, I'm sure.

Shall I wash your face now, ma'am?

ANNE. Yes, please.

ABIGAIL *takes up a bowl of water and a cloth and begins to do so with great care.*

ABIGAIL. I saw a woman earlier today, about the laundry job. I thought she seemed quite suitable.

ANNE. That's good. What is her name?

ABIGAIL. Lassiter. A widow. She told me such a tragic tale. Her husband died at Blenheim. Her eldest son is also at the war, but there's been nothing from him now for months. She thinks he must have fallen too. Another son just lost his job and so has been recruited – forcibly. Though he is very sensitive, she says. Her youngest son... perhaps I shouldn't say it.

ANNE. Do.

ABIGAIL. He didn't want to go, ma'am. He has a little wife, and she's with child. He cut across the sinews in his legs, below the knees. But the sergeants heard of what he'd done and now he's put in gaol for it and like to hang. It struck me as so very sad. And then she said that none of them had known what they were fighting for – not properly. Except to beat the French, of course, but now all say that's done. It struck me as so very sad.

Pause. ANNE *is thinking.*

ANNE. Did you offer her the post?

ABIGAIL. I told her I would speak to you.

ANNE. Offer it.

ABIGAIL. I will then, ma'am. And she'll be very glad of it, for she is lately put onto the streets.

There now. I'll comb your hair for you.

ABIGAIL *sets aside the bowl of water and taking up a comb, begins to comb* ANNE*'s hair.*

ANNE. I delivered seventeen. Though some weren't fully… formed. I remember well how each one felt inside me. I used to wonder what God meant. To take them all. I won't have any more…

ABIGAIL. Ma'am…

ANNE. I won't. I think that's clear. But I am mother to a nation now. That was always His intent.

I lose too many sons.

ABIGAIL. You do.

Pause.

ANNE. But forgive me. You cannot want to talk about such things, I'm sure.

ABIGAIL. Don't worry.

ANNE. Do you feel your baby move?

ABIGAIL. Oh, yes. And see him too. A heel perhaps. Sometimes an arm.

ANNE puts her hand on ABIGAIL's tummy. ABIGAIL is very still.

ANNE. George and I would like to be his godparents. If that would please you?

ABIGAIL. Very much.

ANNE. We'll keep him safe.

ABIGAIL kisses ANNE's head.

ABIGAIL. Where would we be without you, ma'am?

Scene Five

HARLEY's *rooms, the Inns of Court. Evening.* RADCLIFFE, DEFOE, JEZEBEL *and* COMPANY *perform a song, which has an increasingly dark and threatening mood.* SWIFT, *the author of the song, is watching on with satisfaction.*

COMPANY.
What a dream I had last night
And woke with heart a-trembling
For all around the town was wrecked
By murderous hordes descending
And here they robbed and there they raped
And truth and hope lay dying
And none dare move to stop the fray
But closed their ears and turned away
Though every soul was crying
Though every soul was crying.

Enter PERFORMERS, *carrying high an effigy of Marlborough in the guise of a knight.*

And there on the hill top in armour of gold
Stood a glorious horseman with countenance bold
And by the sun's fire on the face of his shield
The words 'Judas Iscariot' plainly revealed
Though mighty and fearsome he never rode down
But smiled as destruction was wreaked all around.

Enter MAYNWARING. *He watches and is immediately alarmed.*

Says I to my neighbour 'Why who is this man
Who stops not the pillage when surely he can?'
Says he, 'That's the hero who once we adored
But now he's in league with the thieves from abroad
And much of the riches they steal are for him
And he's building a temple to squander them in.'

SWIFT. Maynwaring. Come to see how it's really done?

Enter JEZEBEL *dressed as Anne in the guise of an angel.*

COMPANY.
Then saw I an angel, the spirit of grace
With majesty etched on her valiant face
Enthroned was she 'neath a vast purple shade
And surrounded by crowds who called blessings and praise
Though patient and steadfast her spirits were rent
And I drew ever closer to hear her lament.

JEZEBEL.
What a dream I had last night
And woke with heart a-trembling.

Enter PERFORMERS, *carrying high a hideous effigy of Sarah in the guise of a Fury. At the same moment,* SARAH *enters, clutching a pamphlet in her hand. There is a sense that she has got wind of what is happening and has come to see for herself.*

COMPANY.
Said I to my guide who had taken my hand
'Why moves not the angel to rescue the land?'
He pointed at once to the place by her side

Where a hideous Fury I quickly espied
And sulphorous smoke from her nostrils did rise
As she poisoned the air with the stench of her pride.

MAYNWARING (*to* SARAH). Your grace. Your grace, I
wouldn't...

But SARAH *shrugs him away and continues to watch,
transfixed and horrified.*

COMPANY.
Her hair was entwined with the souls she had wrecked
And the gold of her victims was strung round her neck
Behold then the mother of evil and ill
And we all are enslaved to the power of her will
And so with the horseman she leads us to hell
And we'll never be free till we've broken their spell.

JEZEBEL.
Oh England, my England fair
I'd gladly die to save you.

COMPANY.
Then rise we at once with the strength of the just
And tear down their temples and raise them to dust
And out to the street let us drag them to die
On the bridge of our fathers we'll hang them on high
Then into the river we'll toss them to drown
And we'll cheer as their poison is washed from the town.

DEFOE. To the bridge with them!

The PERFORMERS *start to move towards the door with the
effigies. Exit* SARAH, *horrified and afraid.* MAYNWARING
*watches her go, alarmed and conflicted as to whether to run
after her.*

SWIFT. Hang them high, boys!

(*To* MAYNWARING.) Still sure you back the winning
horse?

MAYNWARING *suddenly rushes to join the*
PERFORMERS *as they move through the door.*

MAYNWARING. Hang them high!

Exit MAYNWARING *and* PERFORMERS. SWIFT *smiles to himself, then follows them.*

Scene Six

ANNE*'s bedroom, St James's. The same evening.* ANNE *and* GEORGE *are in bed.* GEORGE *is having an attack of asthma. He is struggling to get enough air into his lungs.* ANNE *awakens from a terrible dream, with tears on her face. She gradually realises that* GEORGE *is struggling.*

ANNE. Oh, George.

GEORGE. Forgive me. I bother you.

ANNE. That doesn't matter.

GEORGE. Perhaps you should be sleeping somewhere else.

ANNE. I won't leave you. You know I won't.

   Shall I call for someone? Do you want the doctor?

GEORGE. No. No. It is gone. It is gone.

ANNE. Sit back, and I'll arrange your pillows. You might do better sitting up.

   He does so. GEORGE *watches her as she sorts his pillows out.*

GEORGE. You have been crying.

ANNE. No. A little.

GEORGE. Why? What are they doing to you now?

ANNE. It's nothing. Only dreams. The only thing that matters is to get you well again.

   Pause. He continues to watch her.

GEORGE. I have been thinking, Annie... I have not protected you as carefully as I should be. I am sorry.

ANNE. George...

GEORGE. I am so often... I am sometimes defeated by the words, and...

ANNE. I would not wish you any other way. Every day they come to me with questions and advice. Every day they talk at me. You have been my open air. My sands that stretch towards the sea. My boundless hills where I can stroll, where I can breathe.

GEORGE. My love. I thank God that I spend my life with you. You are so strong. You are so wise.

ANNE. You think I am?

GEORGE. Though you are such a little tree, your roots grow deep into the ground. They cannot ever push you down. You are more strong than any of them.

GEORGE *closes his eyes.* ANNE *takes his hand. She is still, and thoughtful.*

Scene Seven

HARLEY*'s rooms, the Inns of Court. Two days later.*
GENTLEMEN, *including* DEFOE *and* MAYNWARING, *are gathered around* SWIFT, *taking up copies of his latest pamphlet.*

DEFOE. But this is excellent, Swift. This will light a fire beneath the Whigs, the like of which they've never seen.

MAYNWARING. Come, gentlemen! Hot off the press! Threepence a piece!

SWIFT. Or free to anyone who'll stand and read it out upon the street!

Enter HARLEY. *He crosses straight to* SWIFT.

Harley. Well met. (*Handing him a pamphlet.*) Your copy, sir.

HARLEY. What is it?

SWIFT. My critique upon the conduct of the allies and the ministry in the prosecution of the war. It's brilliant – even by my standards.

HARLEY. I'm sure it is. By Jove, it's long.

SWIFT. I had a lot to say. The words came flowing out of me like piss after the night before.

HARLEY *draws* SWIFT *away from the crowd.*

HARLEY. Prince George is dead.

SWIFT. Is he, indeed?

HARLEY. Abigail sent word to me.

SWIFT. Let's hope that God speaks Danish.

HARLEY. Her Majesty will be bereft. Alone.

SWIFT. Susceptible is what you mean.

HARLEY. I've just been with the Committee for Accounts. It goes our way. It's like a dream. I think the time has almost come to launch our last, decisive strike. What say you, Swift?

SWIFT. Yes, I agree. Go forth, my friend. My friend, go forth. Fulfil your waiting destiny.

A bell begins to toll.

HARLEY. There's the bell.

I'll go to her as soon as she'll receive me.

HARLEY *starts to leave –*

SWIFT. I dare say you'll be giving up these rooms?

HARLEY. Why so? I hadn't thought to.

SWIFT. You will not want to mingle with us fellows here once
    you are so much with the Queen. You cannot rule two Courts
    at once. Much as it delights my heart to have one of our own
    succeed. It's you who we'll be watching now.

HARLEY. Yes. No. Perhaps. Well. We shall see.

Exit HARLEY.

Scene Eight

The reception room, the Queen's apartments, St James's. ANNE
*is standing alone. Though dressed in mourning black, she looks
regal, and more impressive than she has ever done.* ABIGAIL,
MASHAM, LADY SOMERSET, LADY CLARENDON *and
various other* LADIES *and* LORDS *are also present.*

Enter HARLEY. *He looks surprised on seeing so many people
in the room. He makes a low bow to* ANNE.

HARLEY. Your Majesty. Thank you for agreeing to receive me
    at such a sad, nay, tragic time.

ANNE. Thank you, Mr Harley.

HARLEY. If the matter were not urgent...

ANNE. I think I know why you have come.

    Pause.

HARLEY. Would you prefer that we converse more privately?

ANNE. No. Too much is done behind closed doors. Please tell
    me what you have to say.

    Pause.

HARLEY. The Commissioners for Public Accounts have concluded their inquiry into the Duke of Marlborough's financial conduct. I'm afraid there are some questions to be raised. Most of them pertaining to a sort of personal commission which it seems he has been charging on contracts relating to supplies. And more seriously, perhaps, he has been demanding something similar from the foreign allies we have paid to send us troops.

ANNE. Do you mean a kind of bribe?

HARLEY. Yes. No. Not a bribe exactly, ma'am. But something in that vein. His current rate, I understand, is two and a half per cent. The money he's accrued from this activity amounts to hundreds of thousands of pounds. The Commissioners are recommending a further Parliamentary Inquiry. We cannot rule out the possibility that criminal charges will be brought. I have come to ask Your Majesty's approval and permission to pursue this sad but necessary course.

Silence. All wait. ANNE *sighs deeply. All wait.*

ANNE. You must do it. No one is above the law. And the Duke must have the opportunity to defend his conduct and his name.

HARLEY. My sentiments precisely, ma'am.

ANNE. I want it doing fairly, Mr Harley. There will be no witch-hunt.

HARLEY. Yes, of course.

ANNE. Do as you would be done by.

Something in ANNE*'s look and words sends a shiver down* HARLEY*'s spine.*

When is he returning from abroad?

HARLEY. Within the week, I understand.

ANNE. It will be a wretched homecoming.

HARLEY. Your Majesty, I am acutely sensible of the pain this matter must occasion you. Though, I think I speak for all the land, when I suggest there's also promise in this day. The

Duke and – yes – the Duchess too have lately proved the major obstacle to peace. Now perhaps, we might...

ANNE. I will move for peace at once. A conference must be arranged, as quickly as is possible. Convene the Cabinet, and Court. I will consider the proposals from the French.

HARLEY. I see. Why, yes. I see. Good Lord.

ANNE. My sovereignty began with war. And by that war has been defined. But that will change. The war is won. I'll see my country flourish now. My reign will move towards the sun.

Scene Nine

The Marlboroughs' house, St Albans. SARAH finishes reading a letter. MARLBOROUGH is standing apart from her.

SARAH. She doesn't say that you're dismissed. Only that you are suspended, pending an inquiry.

MARLBOROUGH. She knows I will not suffer that. I will resign at once and with immediate effect.

SARAH. But why? You can't. There is no need. Allow this travesty of an inquiry to play out, and in the meantime we can work to...

MARLBOROUGH. She moves for peace. It is confirmed. And I'm the last to know, it seems.

SARAH. She might arrange some talks. But she can do no more than that. You know our allies won't accept the terms the French are offering.

MARLBOROUGH. She abandons all our allies. She breaks all treaties signed. She will have peace at any price.

SARAH. Who told you this?

MARLBOROUGH. Godolphin. Others. And if you'd been attending Court you would have known it too.

SARAH *is shocked*.

We have to leave. We have to go abroad at once.

SARAH. No. She's doing this to caution you. To caution me. Yes – there's the point, I think. It's done to clip my wings.

MARLBOROUGH. We'll go to Antwerp. Then to Hanover. I'll find no shortage of support. Then let the pale Pretender come. Does she think he'll write to her and ask her for permission? Or wait until she's in her grave? Let him come. And when she's tamed and set aside, and British lungs are choked with incense once again, then I, with Hanover invade. And finish them. These Stuarts have outlived their use. They don't deserve these people. They don't deserve their sacrifice. My God... the blood and bones we left behind.

SARAH. John... you are too hasty. This is wrong. I went too far with her. I see that now. I struck too deep. But this can still be remedied. I'll go to her. Apologise – it's what she wants. I promise you, one word of love, one tender look from me, and she will then be ours again...

MARLBOROUGH. Not everything is done for you. You really think... you are deluded... you really think that this is done as vengeance for some bickering on your behalf?

SARAH *is taken aback and hurt by this*.

Tell the servants that we close the house.

SARAH. That's some new contempt. I never heard that note before. You were not so dismissive of my influence when I was building your career.

Pause.

MARLBOROUGH. Close the house. And tell the servants not to speak to anyone. I don't want it reported that we go.

SARAH. No. I will not leave. I will not run or sneak away...

MARLBOROUGH. I can't go back into the Tower! I cannot let it end that way.

SARAH. But you won't have to. Why aren't you hearing me? The charges which they bring are wrong. Let them put you in a court...

MARLBOROUGH. Not all of them. Not all of them.

SARAH *stares at him*.

Don't look like that. You knew. You are too beady with accounts to claim that it was otherwise. Some of the money... I used to pay for gathering intelligence. Legitimately.

My secretaries will vouch for that. Many people can. But some of it...

SARAH. Where has it gone?

MARLBOROUGH. Oh, you know where. Into that monstrosity in Oxfordshire. It's bricked into the walls. We could have built a home. But no, we must have Vanbrugh, and colonnades, and marble brought from Italy...

SARAH. You wanted those things more than I. You saw the plans. So this is my fault after all?

MARLBOROUGH. I blame myself. For thinking myself better than I am. For playing Duke.

SARAH. That's what she wanted...

MARLBOROUGH. We don't have time for this. Start packing up. Write to the girls...

SARAH. Just give me chance to speak to her. I promise you...

MARLBOROUGH *starts to leave*.

Where are you going?

MARLBOROUGH. The bank. To take our money out before they do.

He stops for a moment.

I'll be back soon. Let no one in whilst I am gone.

Exit MARLBOROUGH.

Scene Ten

The reception room, the Queen's apartments, St James's.
SARAH *is sitting on a stool, waiting. She has waited for some*
time. Enter LADY SOMERSET, *passing through to the*
Queen's chamber. She takes no account of SARAH.

SARAH. Lady Somerset?

LADY SOMERSET. Yes?

SARAH. How much longer will I have to wait?

LADY SOMERSET. I cannot say, your grace. I told her that
you're here.

SARAH. I start to feel like some Scots lady with a petition.

LADY SOMERSET. I hope she won't be long.

> *Exit* LADY SOMERSET *into the bedchamber.* SARAH
> *waits. She hears laughter from another part of the Palace.*
> *Then all is quiet again. After a few moments,* ANNE *enters.*
> *She is beautifully and regally dressed.* SARAH *sees her and*
> *stands. She makes* ANNE *a deep curtsy.* ANNE *says nothing.*

SARAH. Your Majesty.

It cheers my heart to see you look so well. I've been so
concerned for you.

ANNE. I cannot stay. They wait for me in Cabinet.

SARAH. Yes.

> *Pause.*

Your Majesty… my dearest Mrs Morley. Where to start?
When you dismissed me… I was distressed, and I was angry
– I admit it. You, more than anyone, know how heated I can
be…

ANNE. Whatever you have to say to me, you may put it in
writing.

SARAH. I… I've said and done some foolish things. I see that
now. And I am sorry. I am truly sorry. But it's only because I

care for you, so very much. Nothing matters to me more than...

ANNE. Whatever you have to say to me, you may put it in writing.

SARAH. Don't do this! Not to me. Talk to me. Shout at me if you desire.

Silence.

The charges which they think to bring against the Duke are cruel. And wrong. And he is brought so low by them. Consider everything he's done. And all for you. Why, on the continent they say he is the greatest General in Christendom, yet here...

ANNE *turns and moves to walk away.*

Don't turn away from me. I beg of you. I beg of you. I cannot live and think us so estranged. How did we come to this?

ANNE. Whatever you have to say to me, you may put it in writing.

ANNE *walks toward the bedchamber.* SARAH *rushes forward and puts herself between* ANNE *and the door.*

SARAH. No. No. No. I cannot let you go from me.

ANNE. I will leave.

SARAH. Give me one word. Let me feel that there is hope. I will work. I will try. You are embedded in my soul.

ANNE (*suddenly*). You had my heart.

Pause.

SARAH. I know. I know. Oh, and I was wrong to treat it carelessly. My dearest, darling Mrs Morley. Anne...

SARAH *reaches out and touches* ANNE.

ANNE. Take your hand off me.

SARAH *does so.* ANNE *looks into her eyes for some moments.*

Good day.

Exit ANNE.

SARAH *is still for a minute. Then she sinks to her knees and weeps profoundly.*

Enter ABIGAIL, *carrying a chamber pot towards the bedchamber. She notices* SARAH, *but continues on her way.* SARAH *gets quickly to her feet, and brushes the tears from her face.*

SARAH. Still carrying the pot, I see.

ABIGAIL *takes no notice of her.*

I suppose you think you've won.

ABIGAIL *stops and looks at her.*

But she'll be gone before too long – one way or another. And you'll be back where you began. And be of no account at all.

ABIGAIL. My husband has been knighted. I am Lady Masham now. Before he was, she sat me down and spoke with me. Asked me if I still could be content to sleep beside her bed at night, upon a pallet on the floor. If I would still hold back her hair when she is retching, wash her feet, and tend her sores. I said I would.

SARAH. Bravo. You sold yourself too cheaply. Lords are ten-a-penny.

ABIGAIL. She's kind. She's wise. She prays, and would do right by everyone.

SARAH. She really has you fooled.

ABIGAIL. We need our Queen. To save us from the likes of you.

SARAH *stares at her.*

SARAH. How history will laugh at your submission. The day will come when people scoff and scratch their heads and say, were there such sheep in England? And I will start my memoirs soon. Upon a terrace, by a lake, I think, I'll sit and write, subservient to no one. And oh, what truths I will bequeath.

ABIGAIL *walks towards the chamber.*

Then all will know how hard I tried. And how my gifts were cast aside.

Exit ABIGAIL.

And where my portrait hangs, admired, they'll stare and say, she was supreme. The bravest soul. The keenest mind. The greatest woman of her time.

End.

MUSIC

Queen Anne - Song 1

Helen Edmundson

Ben Ringham

Moderate 2 ♩. = 96 (aiming for!)

George   Anne

To night? To night it has to be, I'm ripe as a cher-ry u-

pon the tree, Pray come and squeeze the pips from me, We'll do it to-night for

Chorus

En - gland. So here's a cheer for Prin - cess Anne, She's do-ing her du - ty the

way she can, She's up and down like a - ny man She's

Helen Edmundson

Queen Anne - Song 2
(Complete update 29 Sept)

Ben Ringham

Anne (all times)

Pri vy___ purse might fall to__ me, I beg__ you to be - stow the key Oh take it, Oh
beg you__ to be - stow on__ me the key__ to all things mi - li - t'ry // Oh take it, Oh
Go vern-ment might fall to__ me, I beg__ you ma'am be - stow the key // Oh take it, Oh

(Probably pause
x 2 & 3 only)

1.2.
poss. poco rall

3.
(Anne)

take it, Oh take_____ it. Your take_____
take it, Oh take_____ it. Your
take it, Oh

Sarah, Marlborough, Godolphin

Queen Anne - Song 3

Helen Edmundson

Ben Ringham

Oh, the Grand Old Duke of Marl - b'rough He
had ten thou-sand men   He marched them up to the top of the hill And none came down a - gain   And
when they were up they were up   And when they were down they were down   And
when they were on - ly half-way up They were fal ling on the ground   Say   you young man What

Bright 2

Marlborough   Old Man

Queen Anne - Song 4

Helen Edmundson

Ben Ringham

Slow 4

BELL NOTES What a dream I had last night And woke with heart a - trem-bling For all a - round the

TACET/UNACCOMP THRU TO BAR 9

town was wrecked By mur d'rous hordes de - scen-ding And here they robbed and there they raped And

PLAY

truth and hope lay dy - ing And none dare move to stop the fray But closed their ears and

turned a-way Though e- v'ry soul was cry-ing Though e- v'ry soul was cry- ing___ And

Quicker
(voice leads)

95 Slow 4 (voice leads)   Quicker (voice leads)

What a___dream I had_ last night And woke with heart a - trem-bling Said I to my

100

guide who had ta - ken my hand 'Why moves not_ the_ an - gel to res - cue the

106

land?' He_ poin - ted at once to the place by her side Where a hi - de - ous

112

Fu - ry I quick - ly e - spied And sul - phu - rous smoke from her nos - trils did

rise   As she poi - soned the__ air with the stench of her pride   Her hair was en -

twined with the Souls she had wrecked   And the gold of__ her__ vic - tims was strung round her

neck   Be - hold then the mo - ther of e - vil and ill   And we all are en -

slaved to the power of her will   And so with the horse-man she leads us to

high   Then   in - to   the   ri - ver   we'll   toss   them   to

drown   And we'll cheer   as___   their   poi - son   is   washed from   the   town

A Nick Hern Book

Queen Anne first published in Great Britain as a paperback original in 2015 by Nick Hern Books Limited, The Glasshouse, 49a Goldhawk Road, London, in association with the Royal Shakespeare Company

Queen Anne copyright © 2015 Helen Edmundson
Music copyright © 2015 Helen Edmundson and Ben Ringham

Cover illustration: *Queen Anne* (1665–1714) (oil on canvas), Wissing, William (1656–87) & Vaardt, Jan van der (1647–1721) / Scottish National Portrait Gallery, Edinburgh, Scotland / Bridgeman Images

Designed and typeset by Nick Hern Books, London
Printed in the UK by CPI Books (UK) Ltd

A CIP catalogue record for this book is available from the British Library

ISBN 978 1 84842 523 1